Classic Myths
Color & Sepia

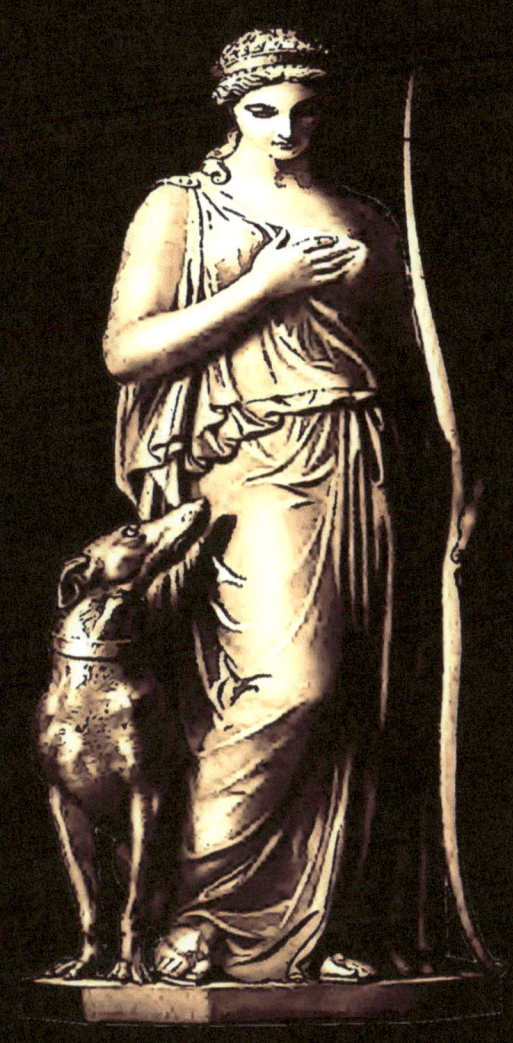

ISBN-13 : 978-1480144644
ISBN-10 : 1480144649

COLOR PLATES

PERSEUS AND ANDROMEDA
From the painting by Lord Leighton, P.R.A., in the Walker Art Gallery, Liverpool

PHOEBUS APOLLO
From the painting by Briton Riviere, R.A., in the Birmingham Art Gallery

THE RETURN OF PERSEPHONE
From the painting by Lord Leighton, P.R.A., in the Leeds Art Gallery

HYLAS AND THE WATER NYMPHS
From the painting by J. W. Waterhouse, R.A., in the Manchester Art Gallery

THE GOLDEN FLEECE
From the painting by H. J. Draper in the Bradford Art Gallery

ECHO AND NARCISSUS
From the painting by J, W. Waterhouse, R.A., in the Walker Art Gallery, Liverpool

CLYTEMNESTRA
From the painting by Hon. John Collier in the Guildhall London

THE LAST WATCH OF HERO
From the painting by Lord Leighton, P.R.A., in the Manchester Art Gallery

Dtp
and
graphic design

Iacob Adrian

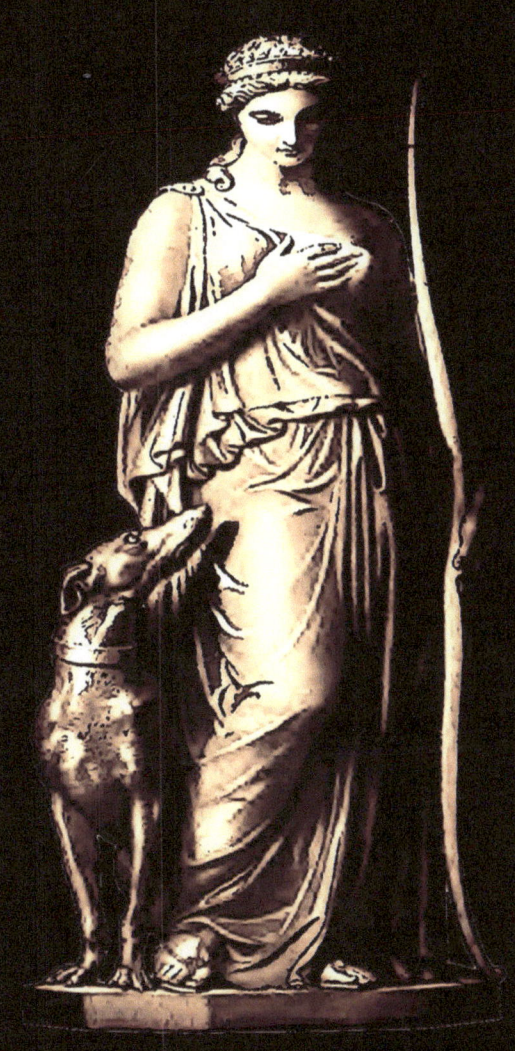

SEPIA PLATES

1. PANDORA. By Dante Gabriel Rossetti.
2. SIBYLLA DELPHICA. By Sir Edward Burne-Jones.
3. ZEUS (JUPITER). From the sculpture in the Louvre, Paris.
4. ENDYMION CONVEYED IN SLEEP TO OLD MOUNT LATMOS.
From the clay relief by Harry Bates.
5. THE VENUS OF MELOS. From the statue in the Louvre, Paris.
6. HERMES CARRYING DIONYSUS. From the statue by Praxiteles.
7. PAN. From the sculpture by Henry A. Pegram, A.R.A.
8. HOMER. From the clay relief by Harry Bates.
9. PERSEUS AND THE GREY SISTERS (GRAIiE). By Sir Edward Burne-Jones.
10. ATALANTA'S RACE. By Sir E. J. Poynter, P.R.A.
11. HERCULES AND THE BOAR. From the bronze by Jean de Bologne.
12. THE GARDEN OF THE HESPERIDES. By Sir Edward Burne-Jones.
13. HERCULES WRESTLING WITH DEATH FOR THE BODY OF ALCESTIS.
By Lord Leighton, P.R.A.
14. ORPHEUS AND EURYDICE. By G. F. Watts, R.A.
15. PROMETHEUS. From the sculpture by Puget.
16. THE LAMENT FOR ICARUS. By Herbert J. Draper,
17. ARIADNE IN NAXOS. By G. F. Watts, R.A.
18. OEDIPUS AT COLONOS. From the sculpture by Hugues.
19. ANTIGONE STREWING DUST ON THE BODY OF POLYNEICES.
By Victor J. Robertson.
20. THE JUDGMENT OF PARIS. By Solomon J. Solomon, R.A.
21. THE PARTING OF ACHILLES AND BRISEIS. By G. F. Watts, R.A.
22. CAPTIVE ANDROMACHE. By Lord Leighton, P.R.A.
23. NEPTUNE. From the sculpture by Adam.
24. LAOCOON AND HIS SONS. From the sculpture in the Vatican Museum.
25. CIRCE. By Sir Edward Burne-Jones.
26. ULYSSES AND THE SIRENS. By Herbert J. Draper.
27. THE RETURN OF ULYSSES. By L. F. Schutzenberger.
28. PENELOPE. After the statue by R. J. Wyatt.
29. PSYCHE AND ZEPHYRUS. From the clay relief by Harry Bates,
30. CUPID AND PSYCHE. From the sculpture by Canova.
31. SAPPHO. By Sir L. Alma-Tadema, R.A.
32. THE THREE FATES. From the painting—" A Golden Thread "—by J.
M. Strudwick.

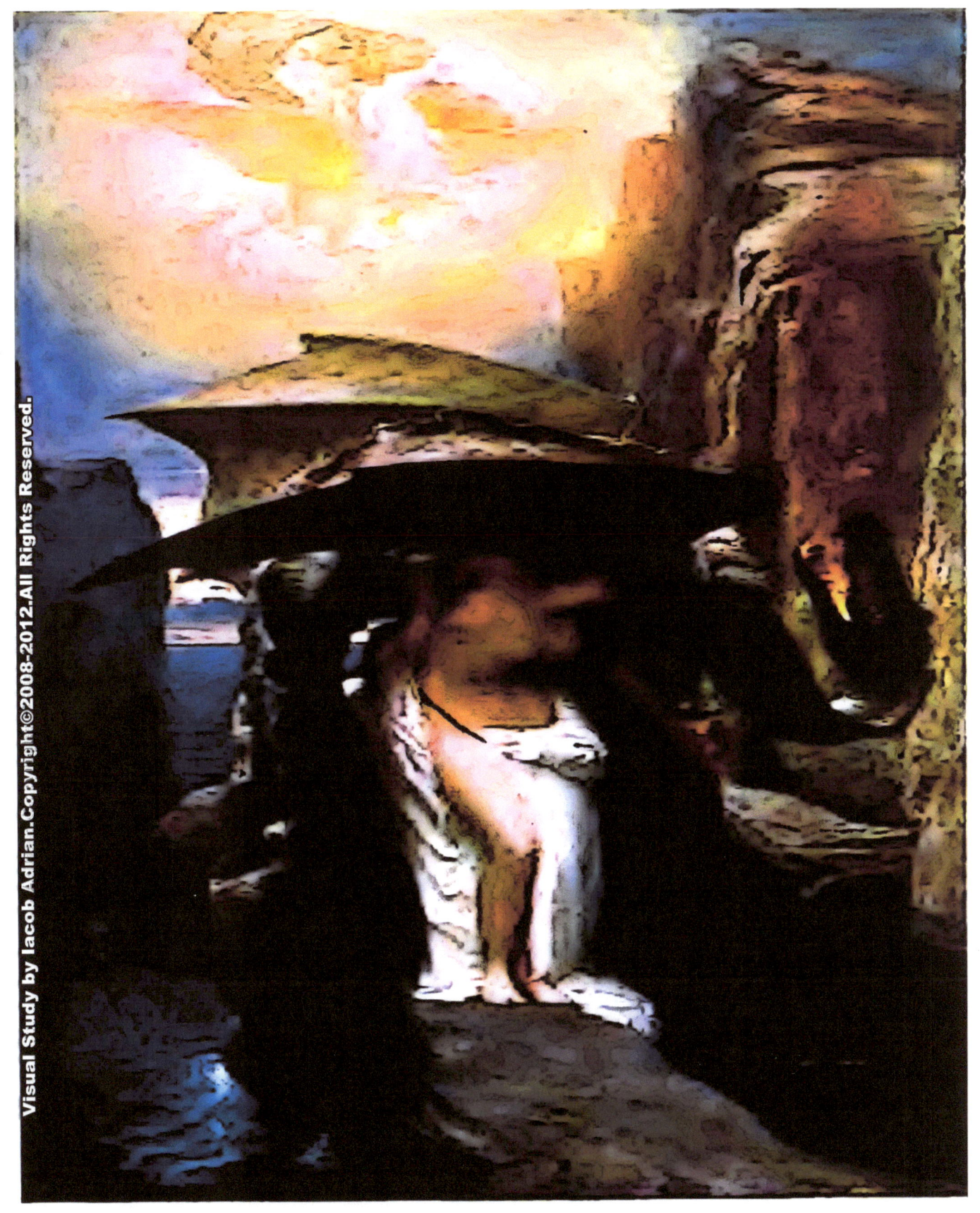

PERSEUS AND ANDROMEDA

From the painting by Lord Leighton, P.R.A., in the Walker Art Gallery, Liverpool

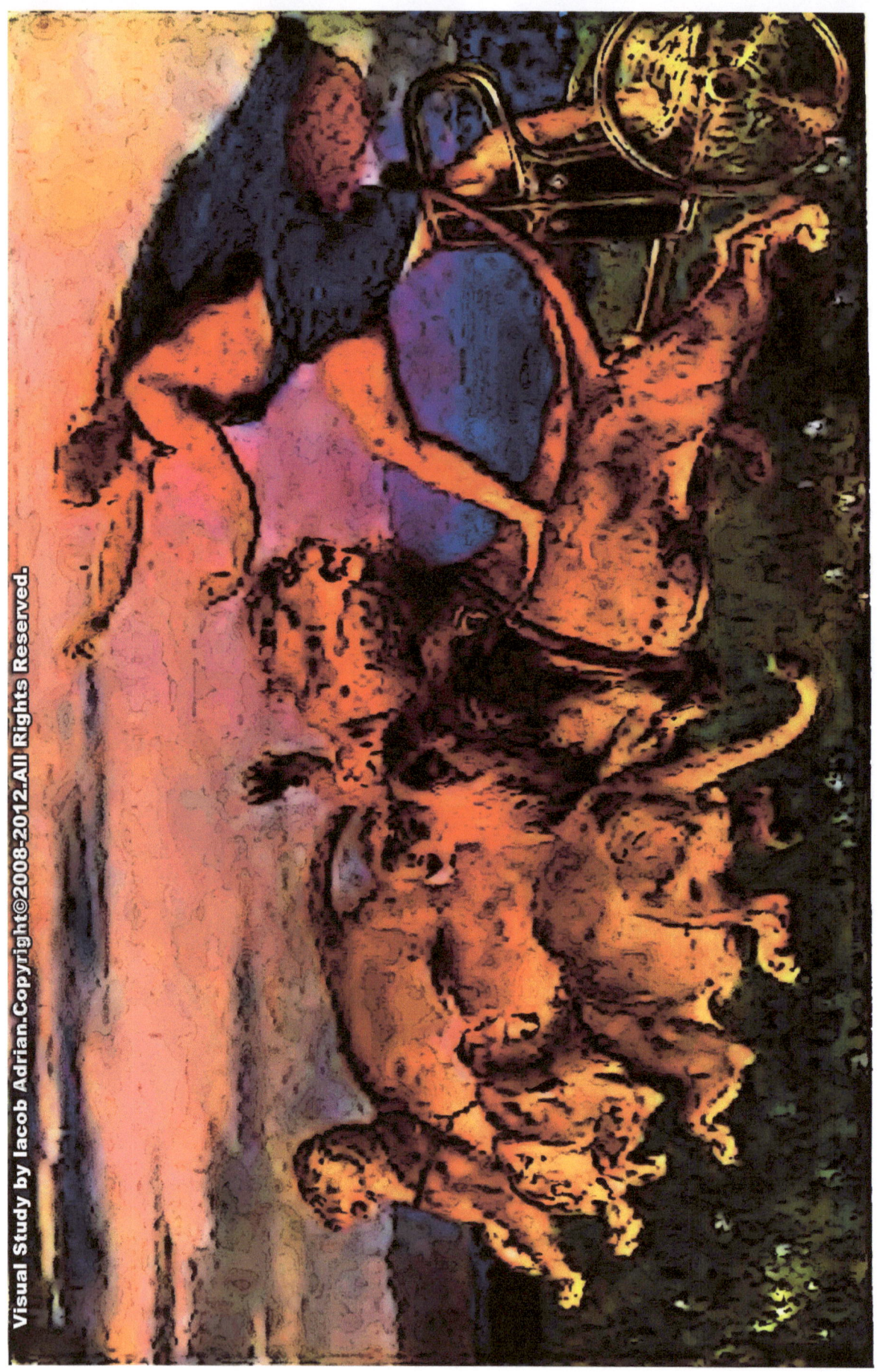

PHŒBUS APOLLO

From the painting by Briton Riviere, R.A., in the Birmingham Art Gallery

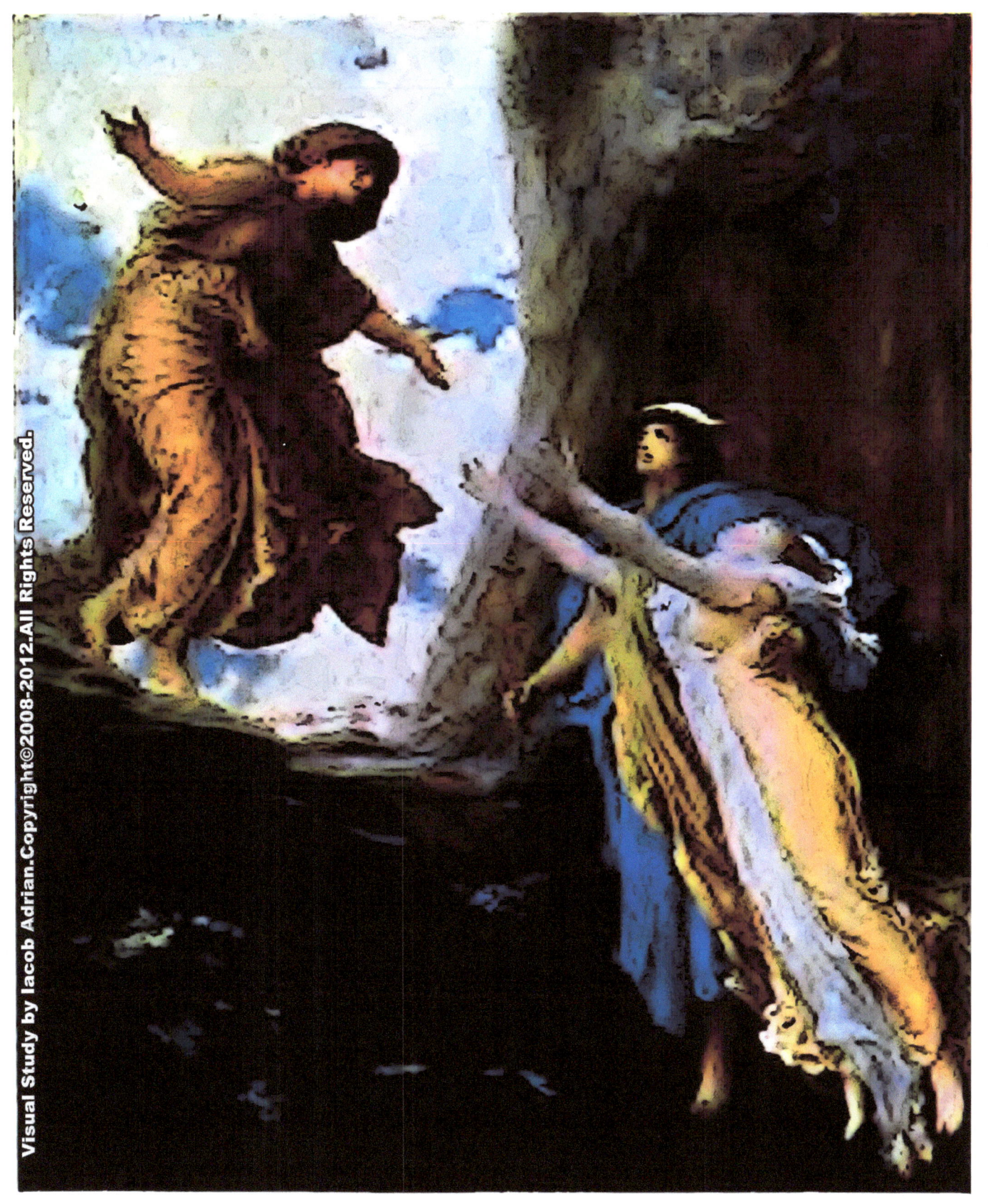

THE RETURN OF PERSEPHONE

From the painting by Lord Leighton, P.R.A., in the Leeds Art Gallery

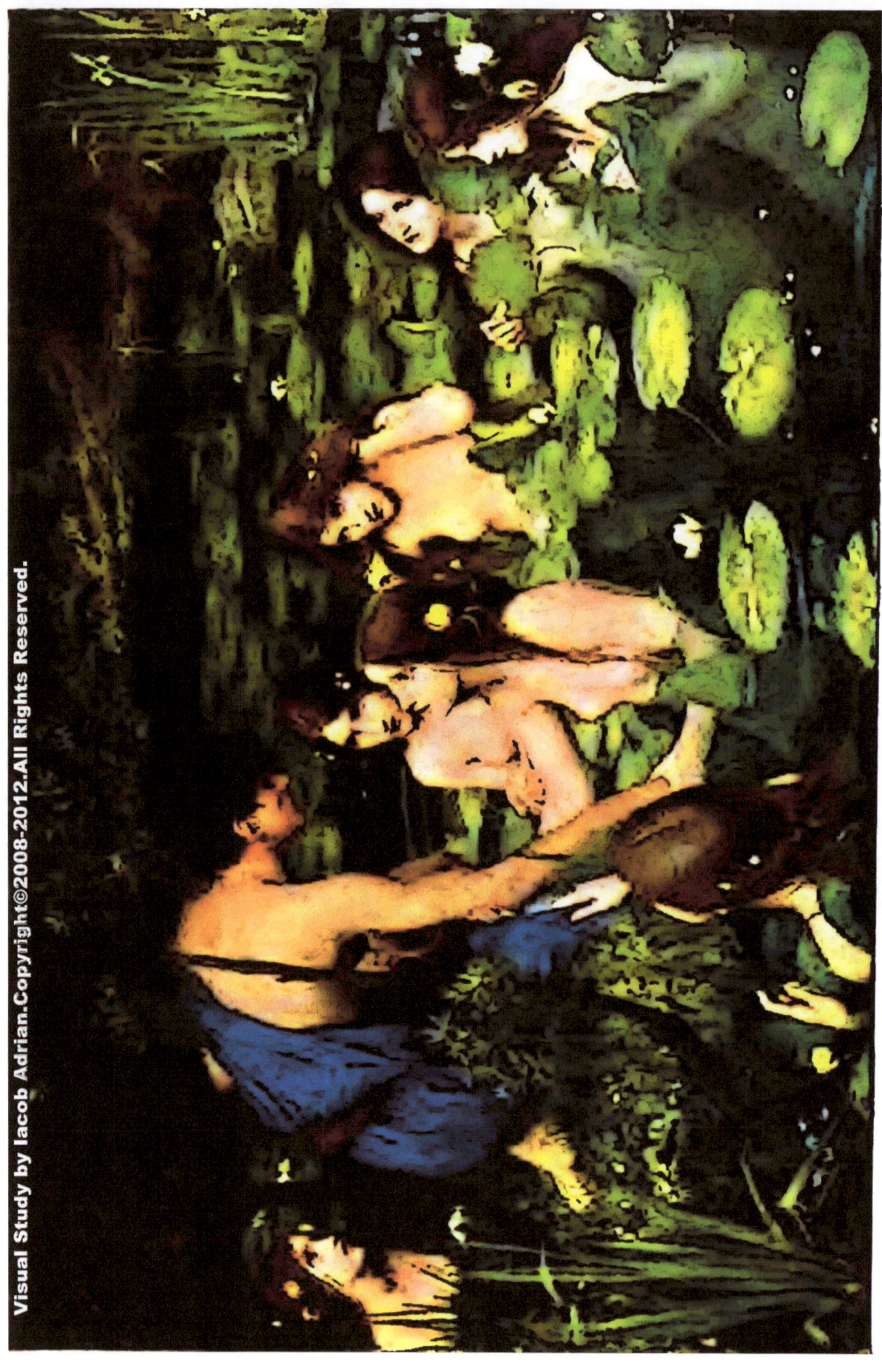

HYLAS AND THE WATER NYMPHS

From the painting by J. W. Waterhouse, R.A., in the Manchester Art Gallery

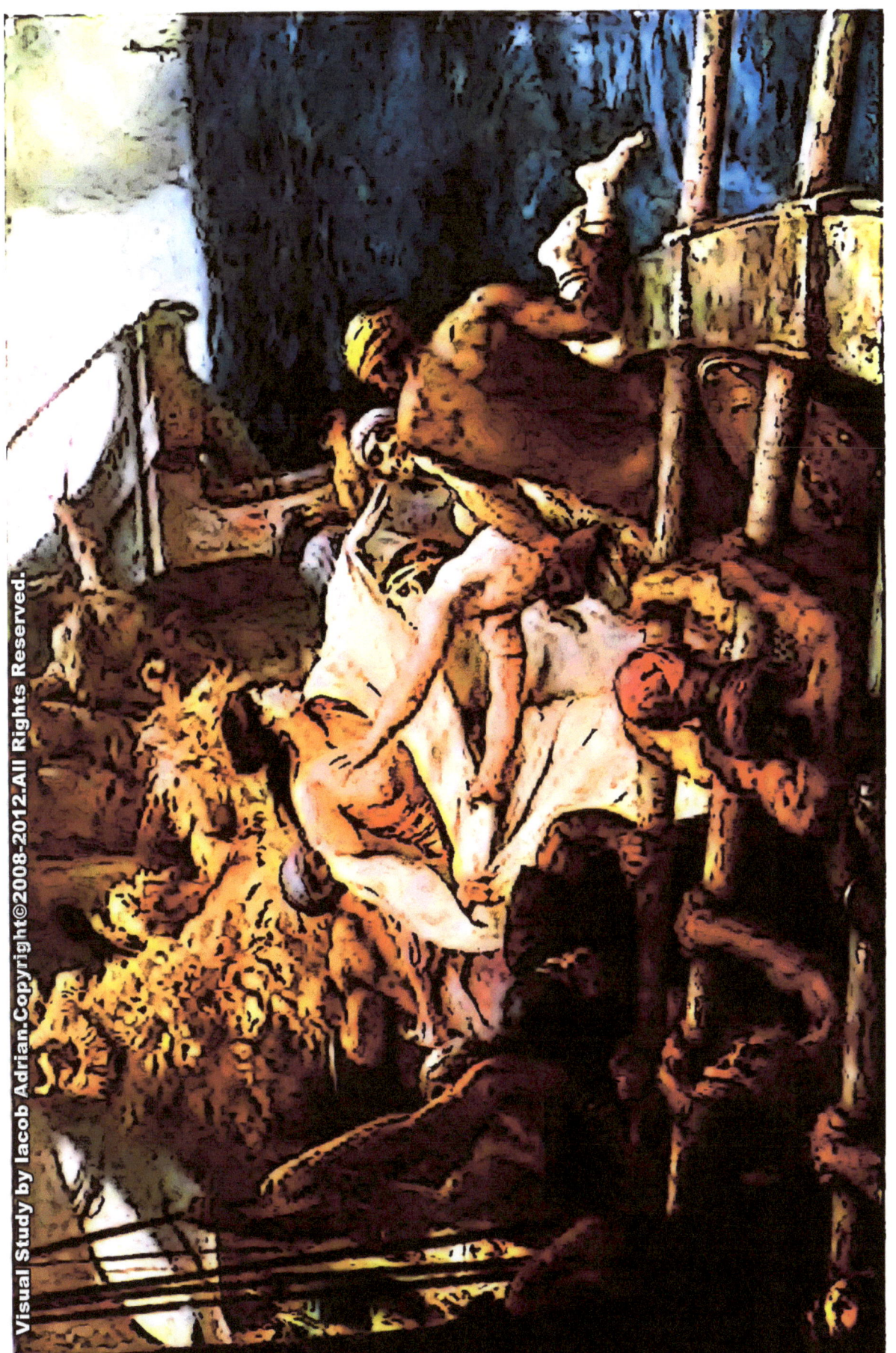

THE GOLDEN FLEECE

From the painting by H. J. Draper in the Bradford Art Gallery

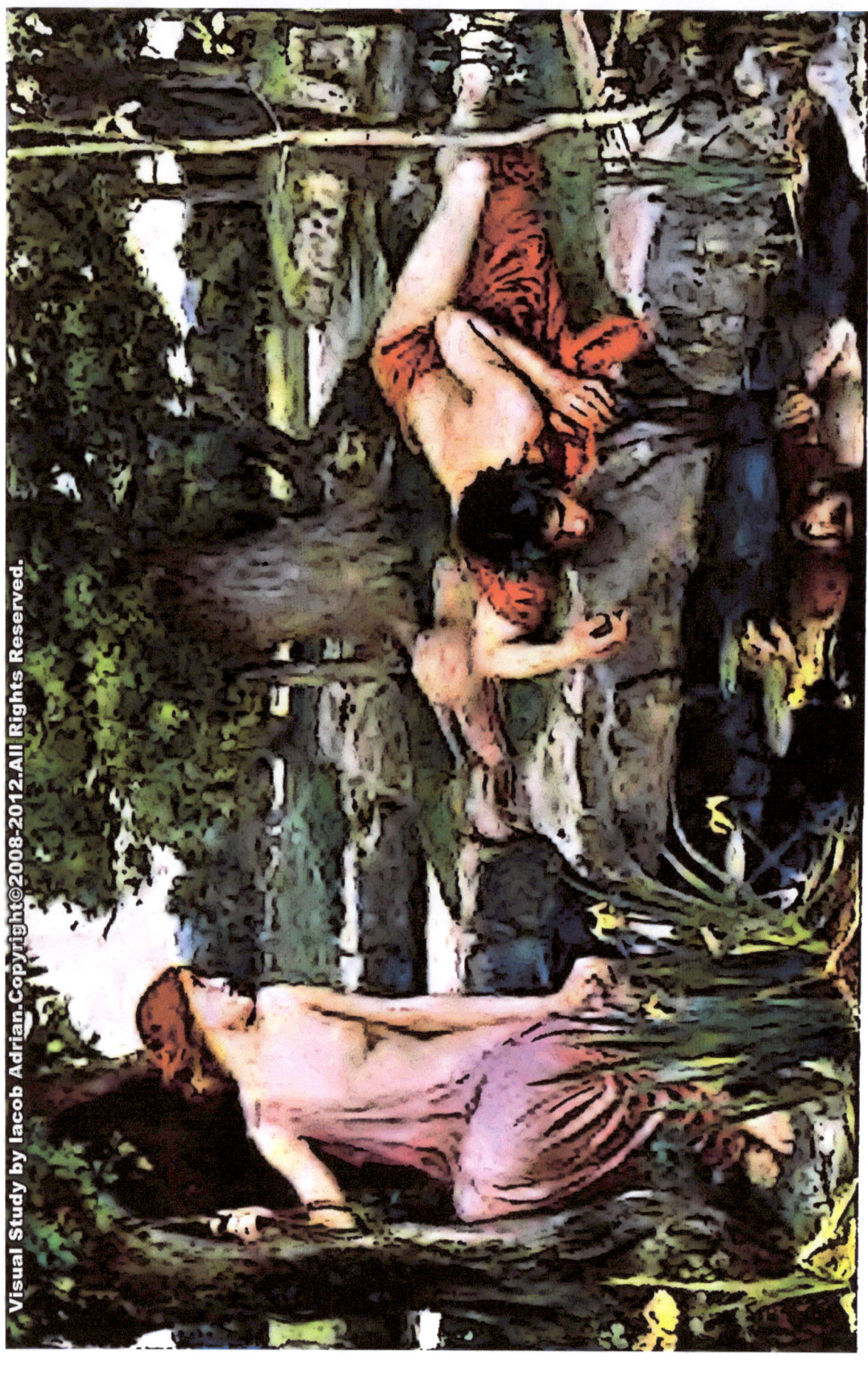

ECHO AND NARCISSUS

From the painting by J. W. Waterhouse, R.A., in the Walker Art Gallery, Liverpool

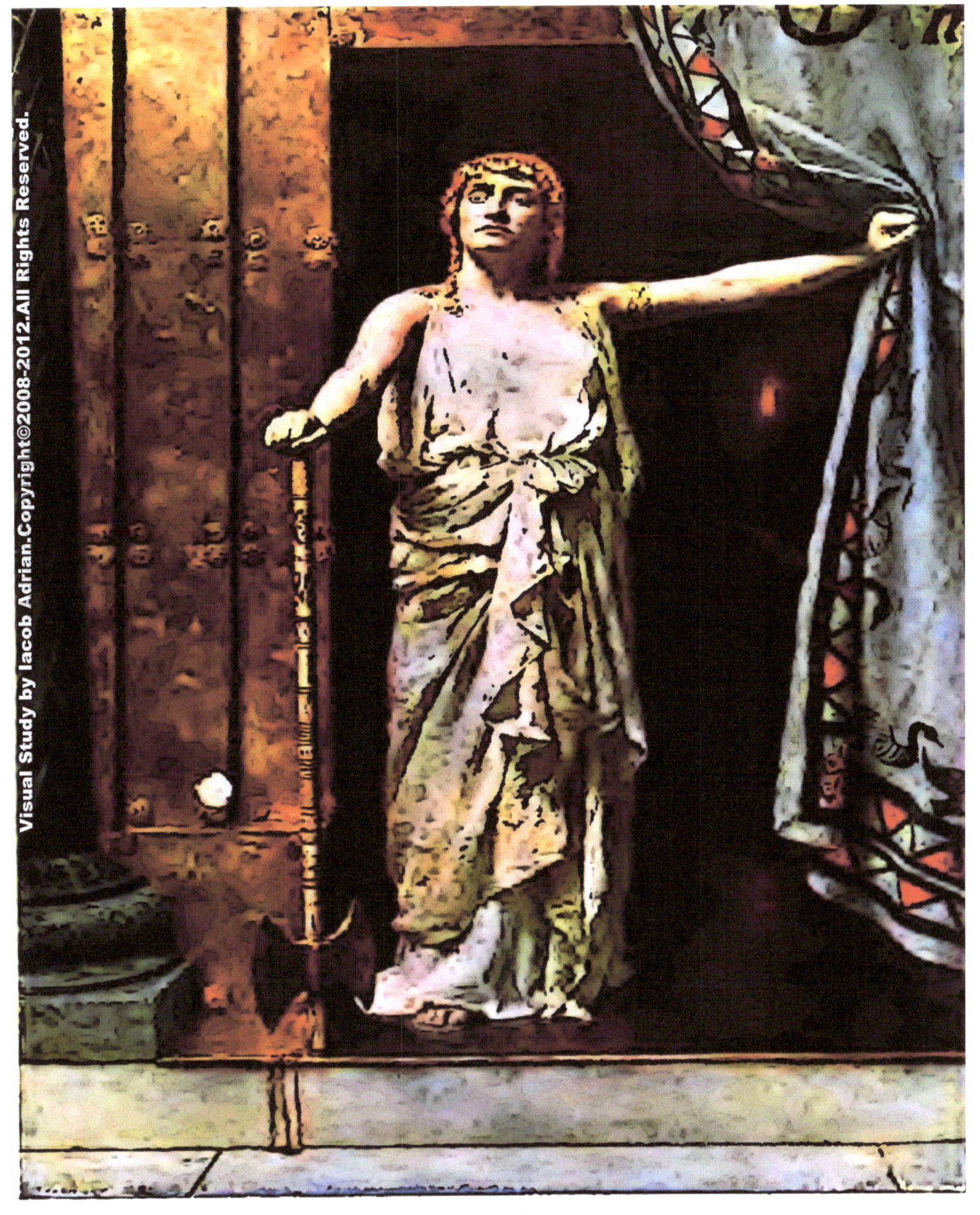

CLYTEMNESTRA

From the painting by Hon. John Collier in the Guildhall, London

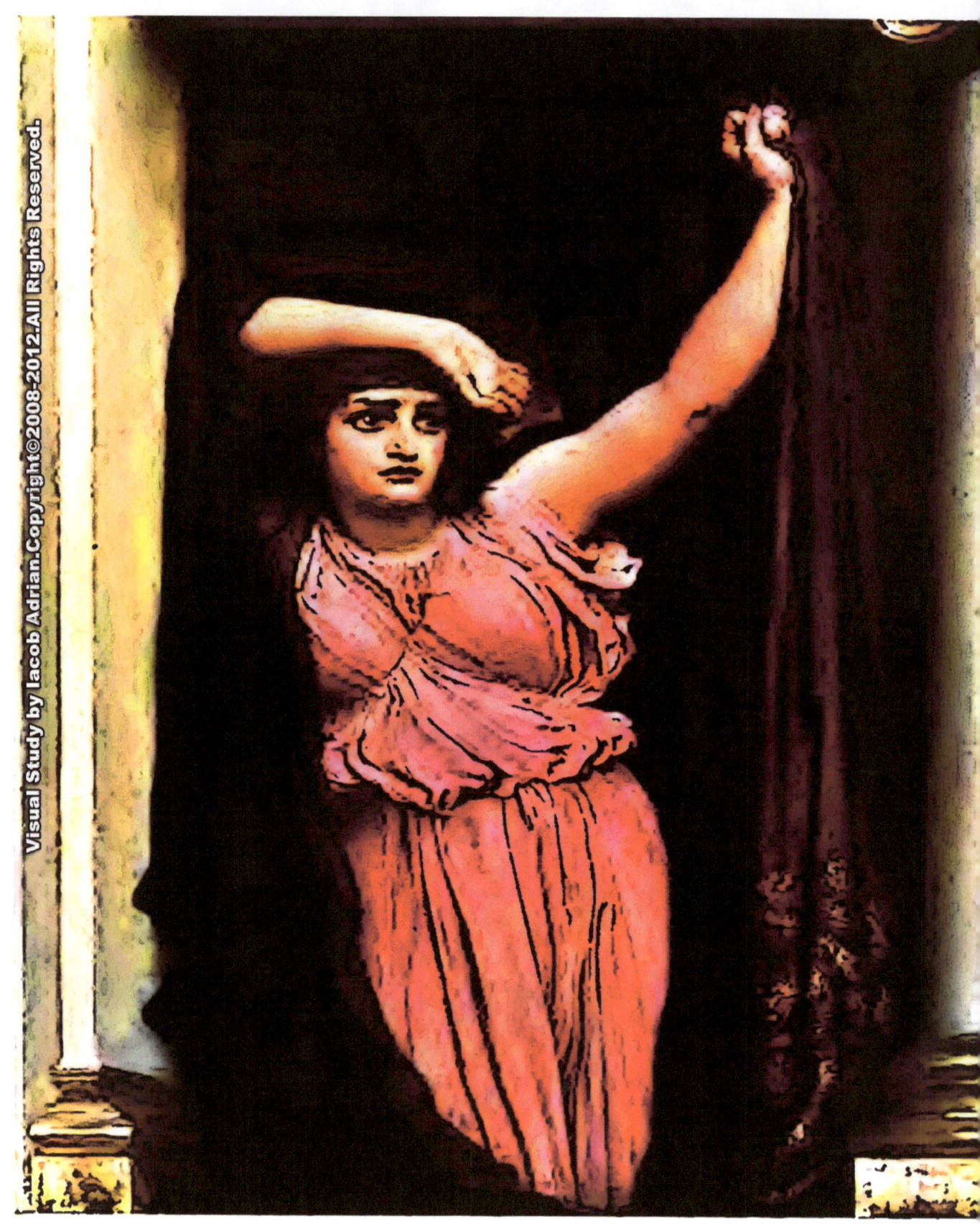

THE LAST WATCH OF HERO

From the painting by Lord Leighton, P.R.A., in the Manchester Art Gallery

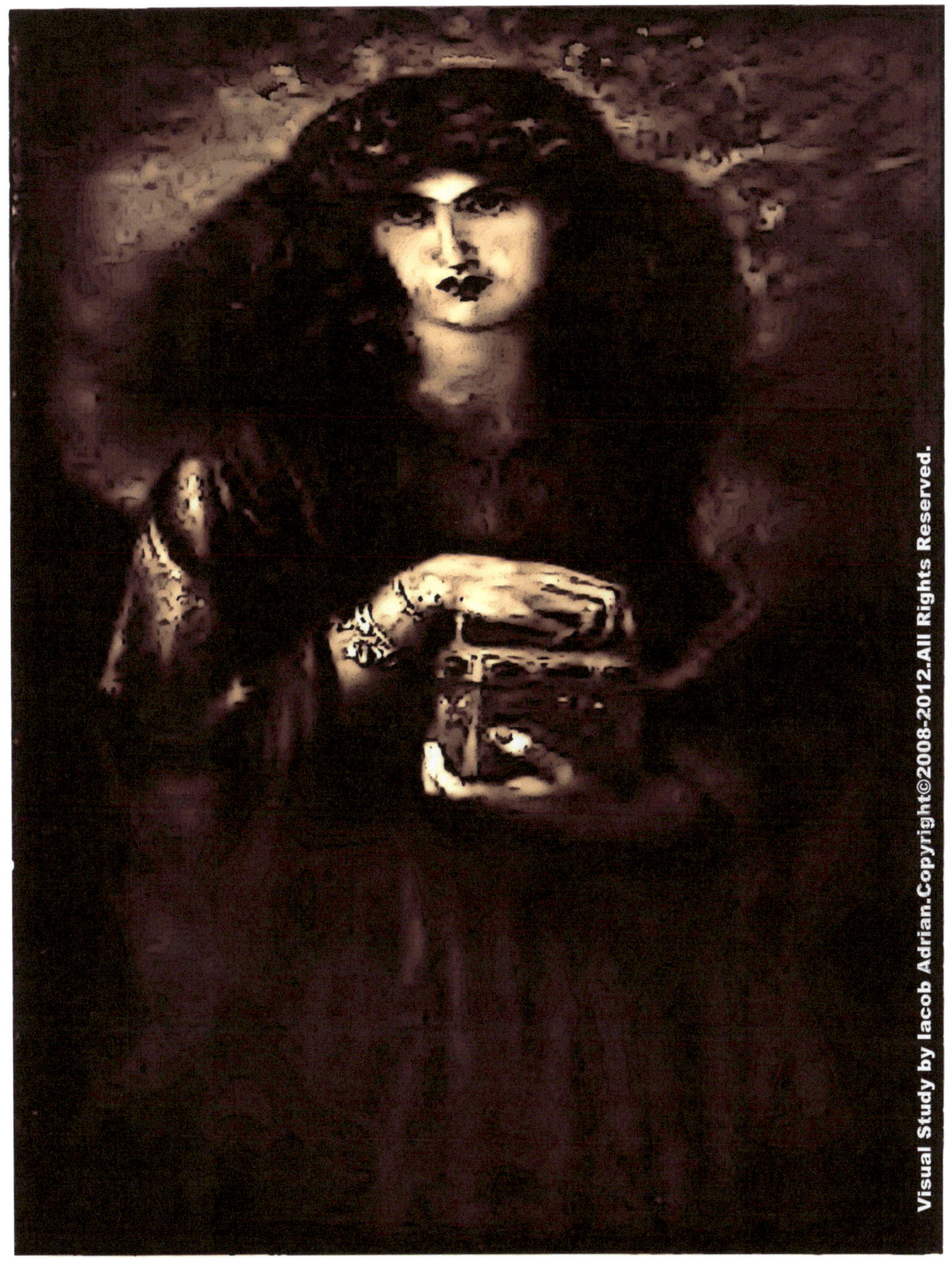

PANDORA
By Dante Gabriel Rossetti

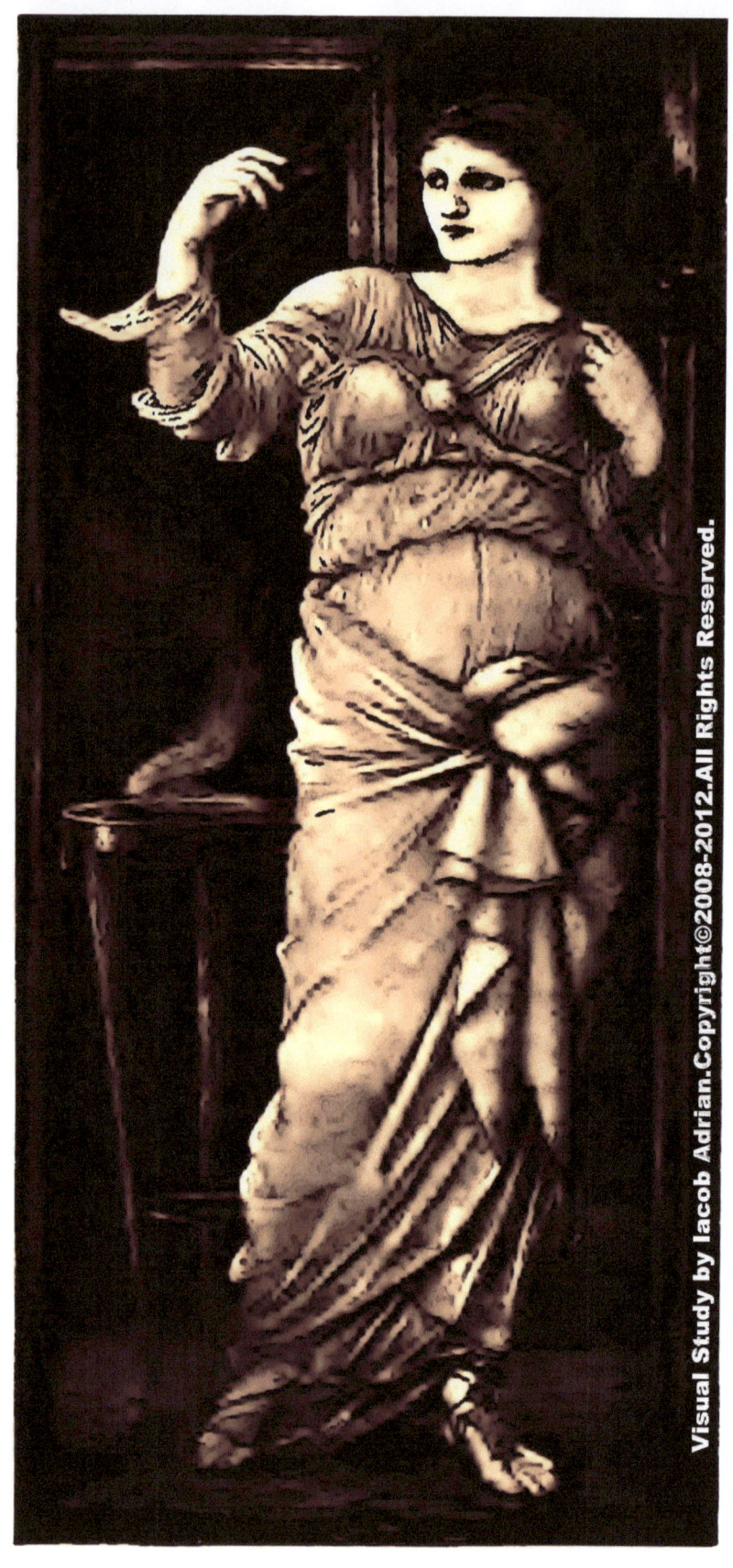

SIBYLLA DELPHICA
By Sir Edward Burne-Jones

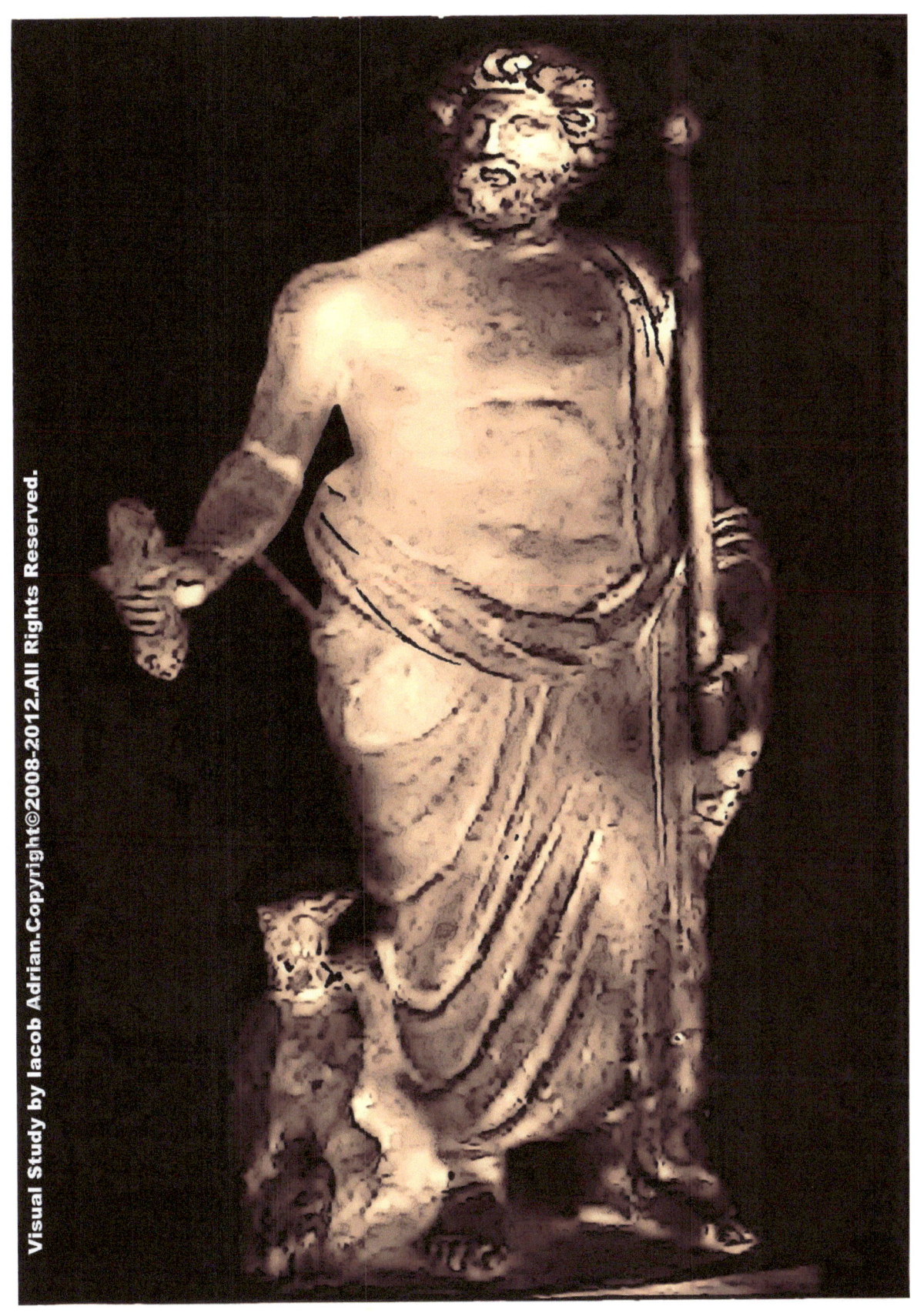

ZEUS (JUPITER)
From the sculpture in the Louvre, Paris

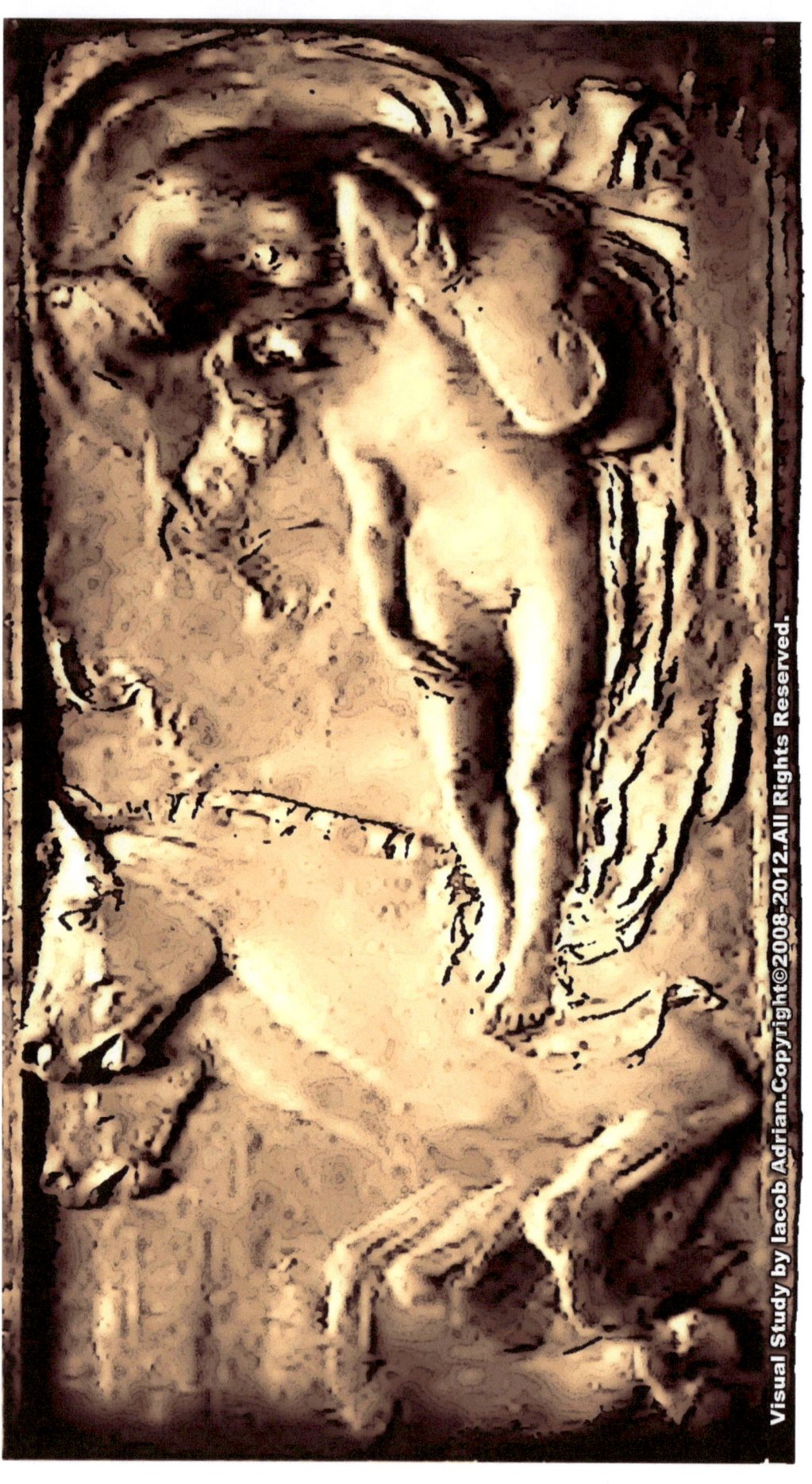

ENDYMION CONVEYED IN SLEEP TO OLD MOUNT LATMOS

From the clay relief by Harry Bates

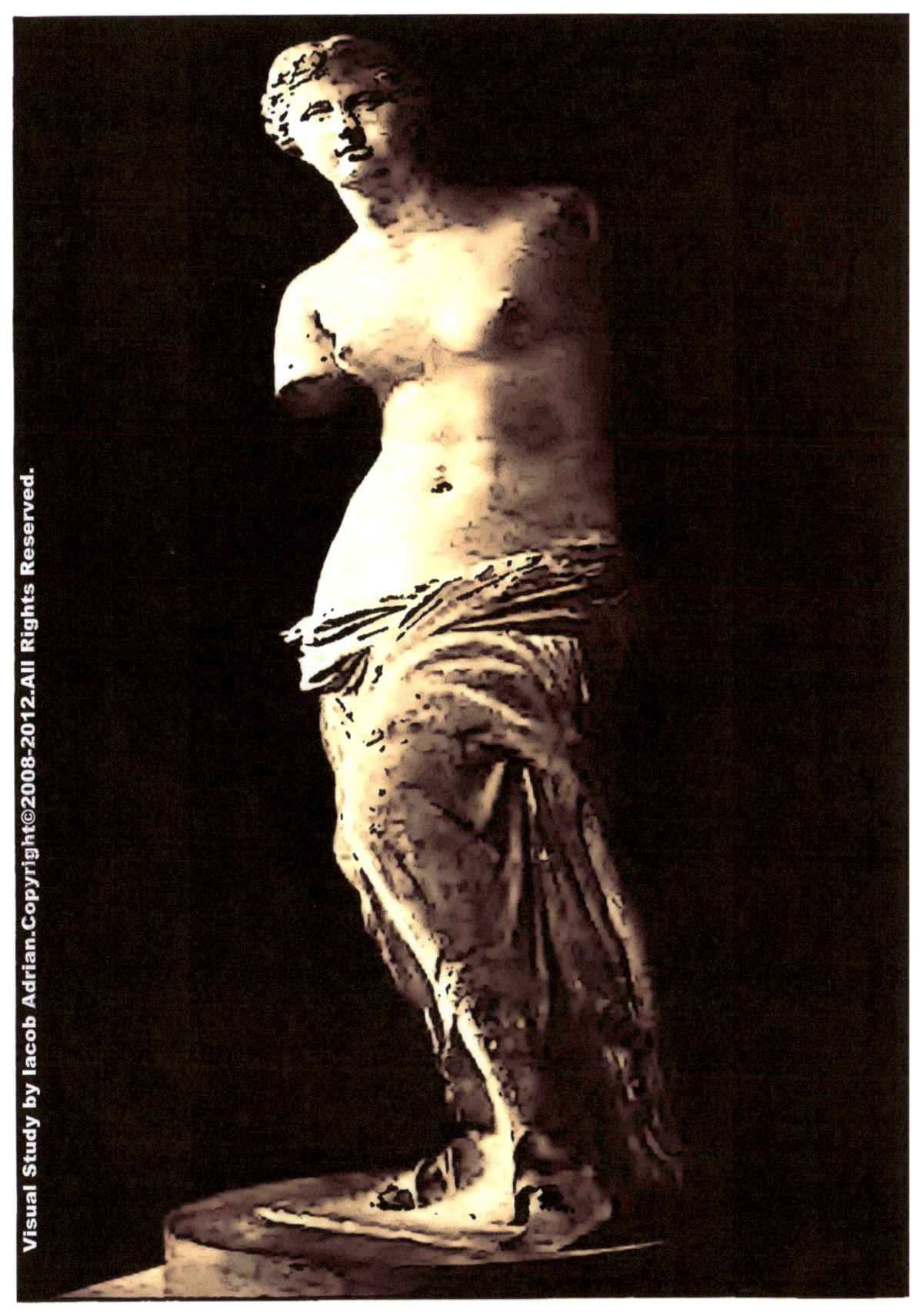

THE VENUS OF MELOS

From the statue in the Louvre, Paris

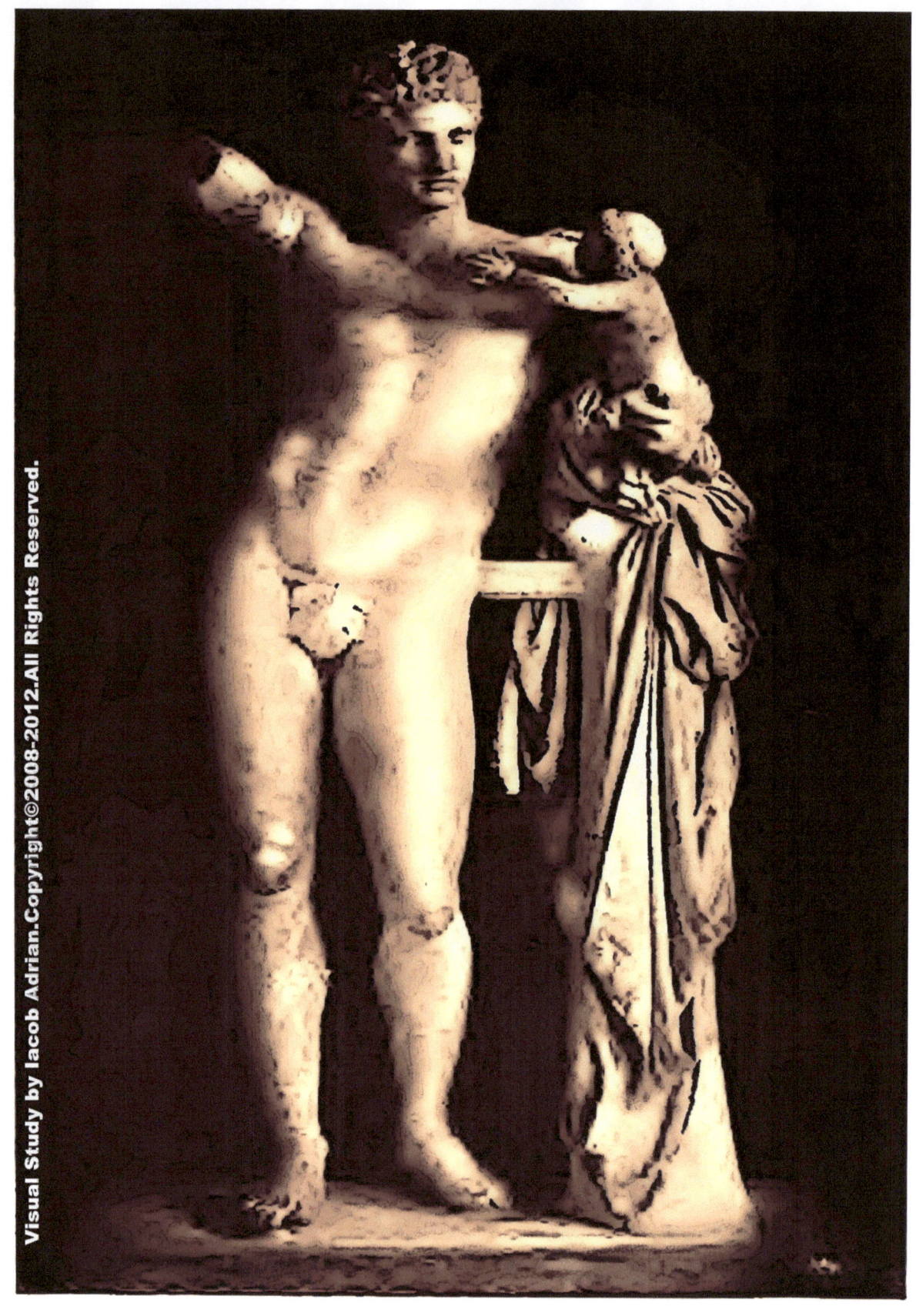

HERMES CARRYING DIONYSUS

From the statue by Praxiteles.   Found at Olympia in 1877

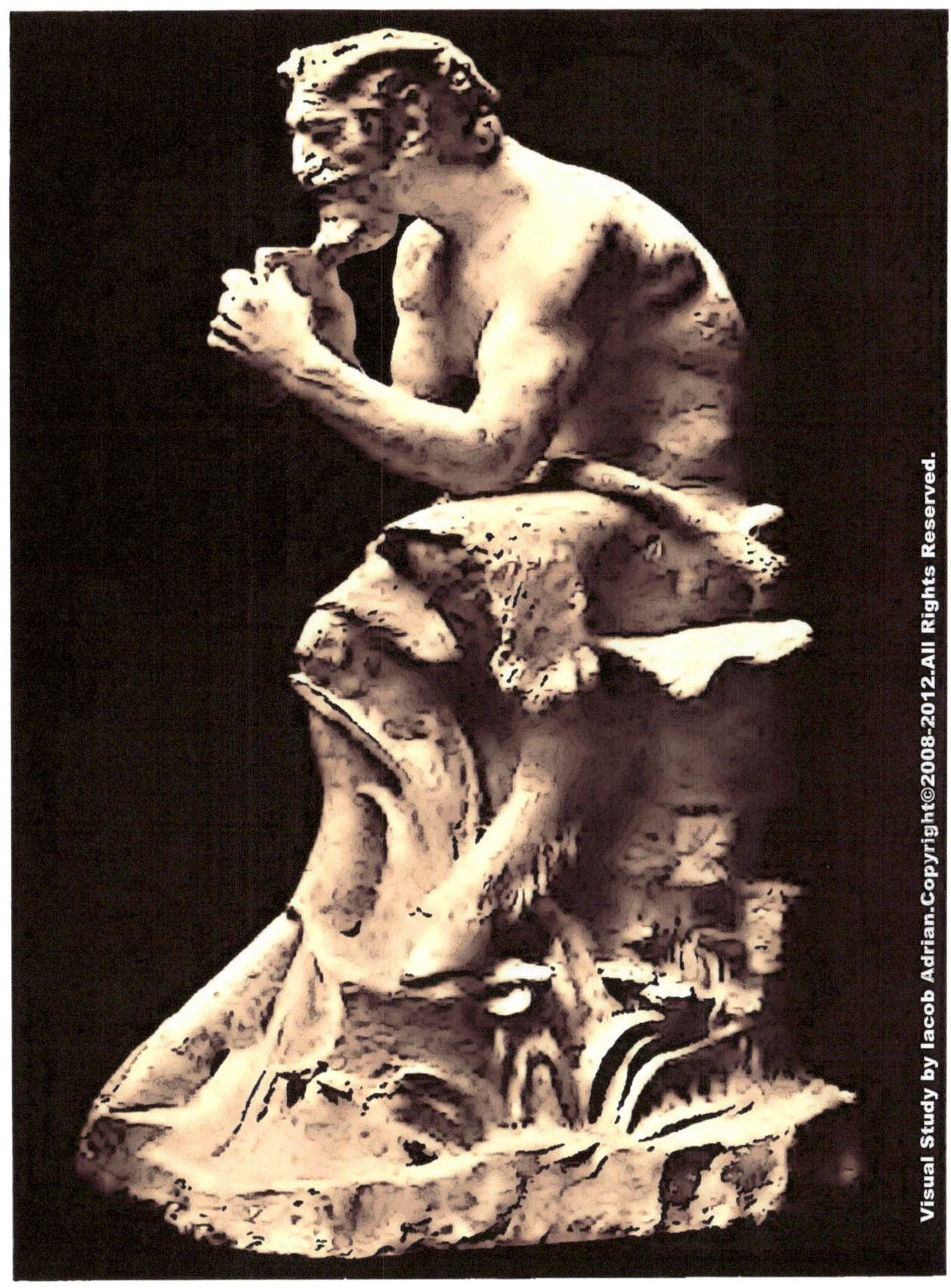

PAN

From the sculpture by Henry A. Pegram, A.R.A.

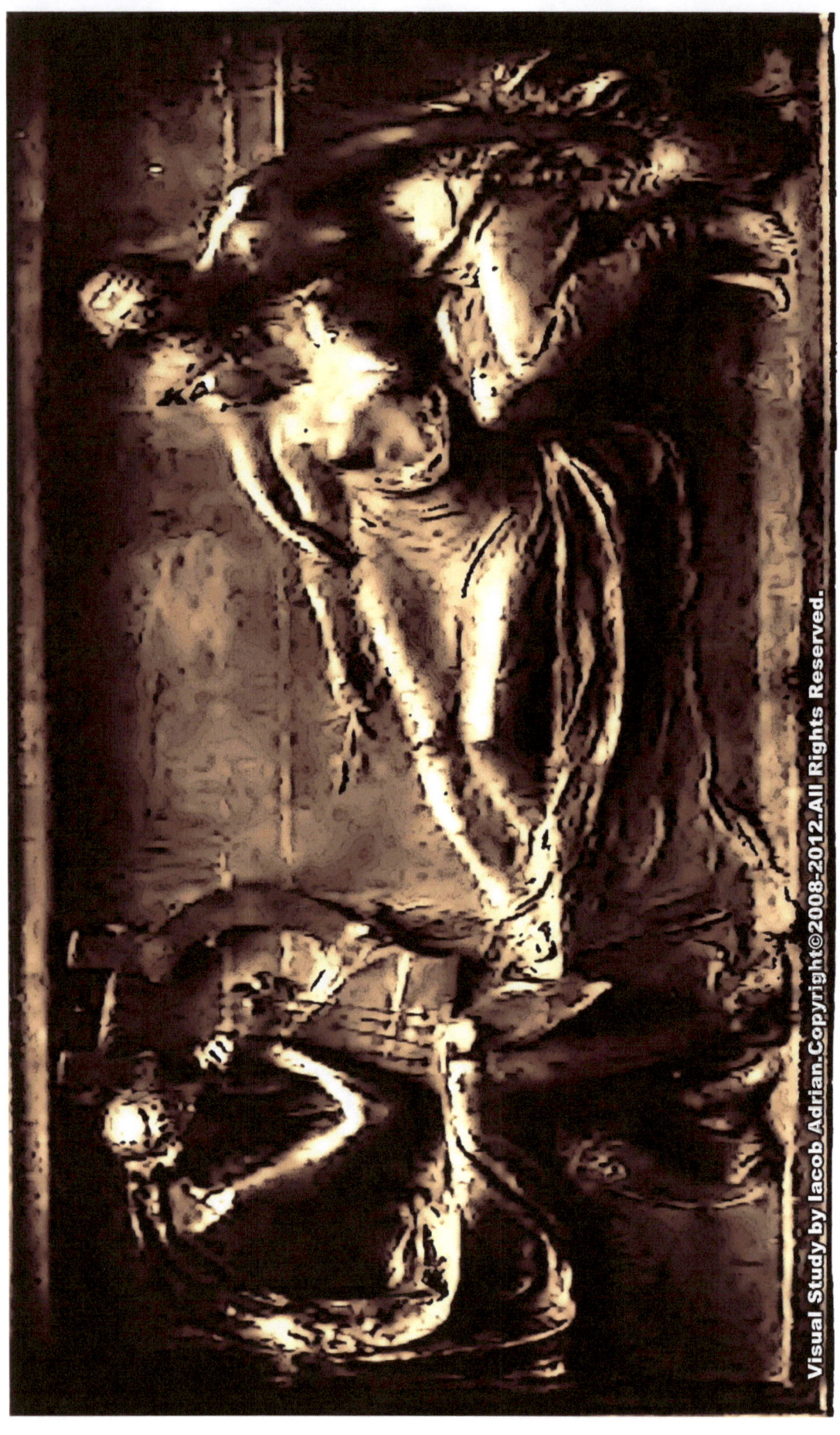

HOMER

(" A blind man, sweetest he sings ")

From the clay relief by Harry Bates

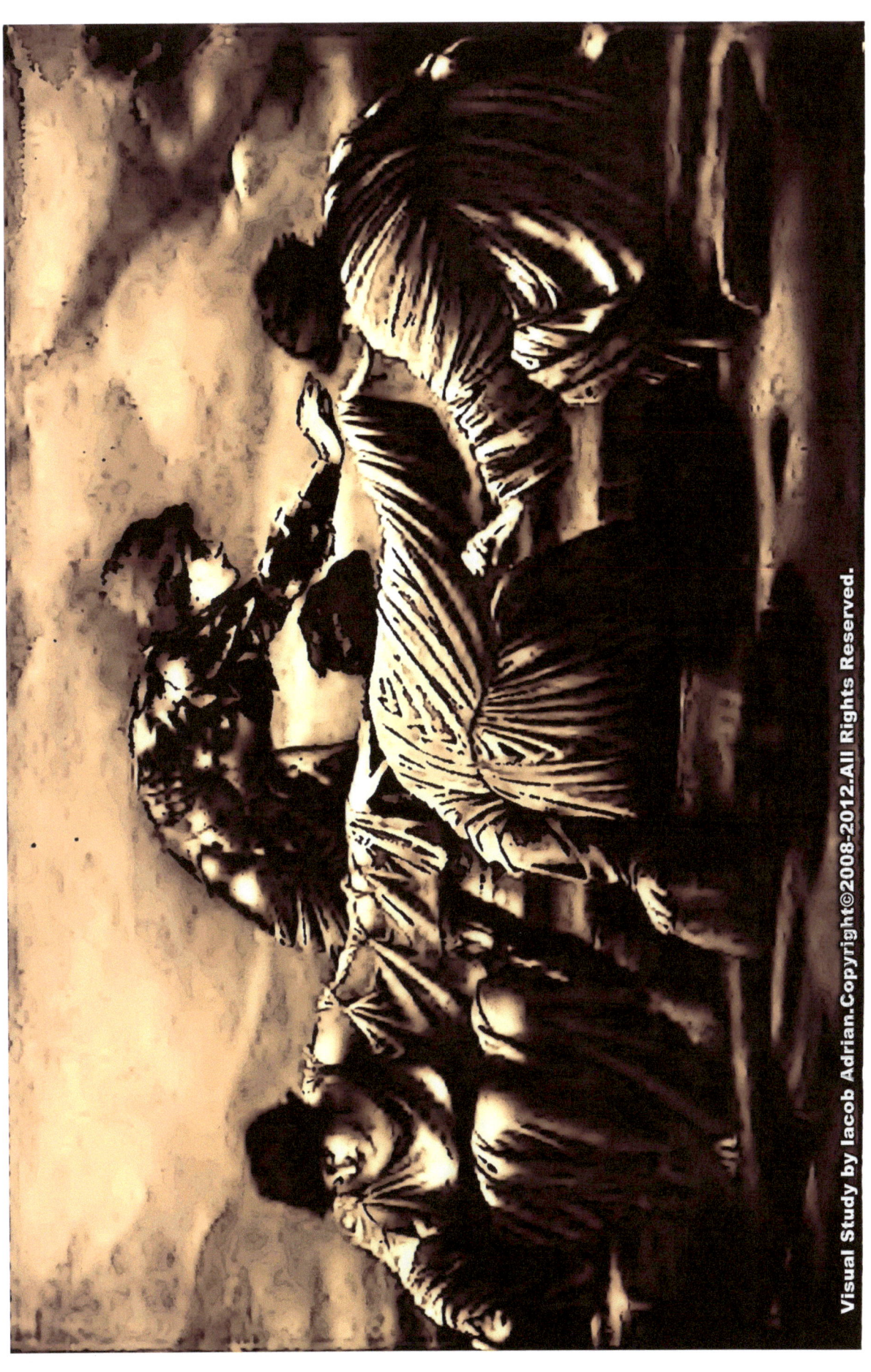

PERSEUS AND THE GREY SISTERS (GRAIÆ)
By Sir Edward Burne-Jones

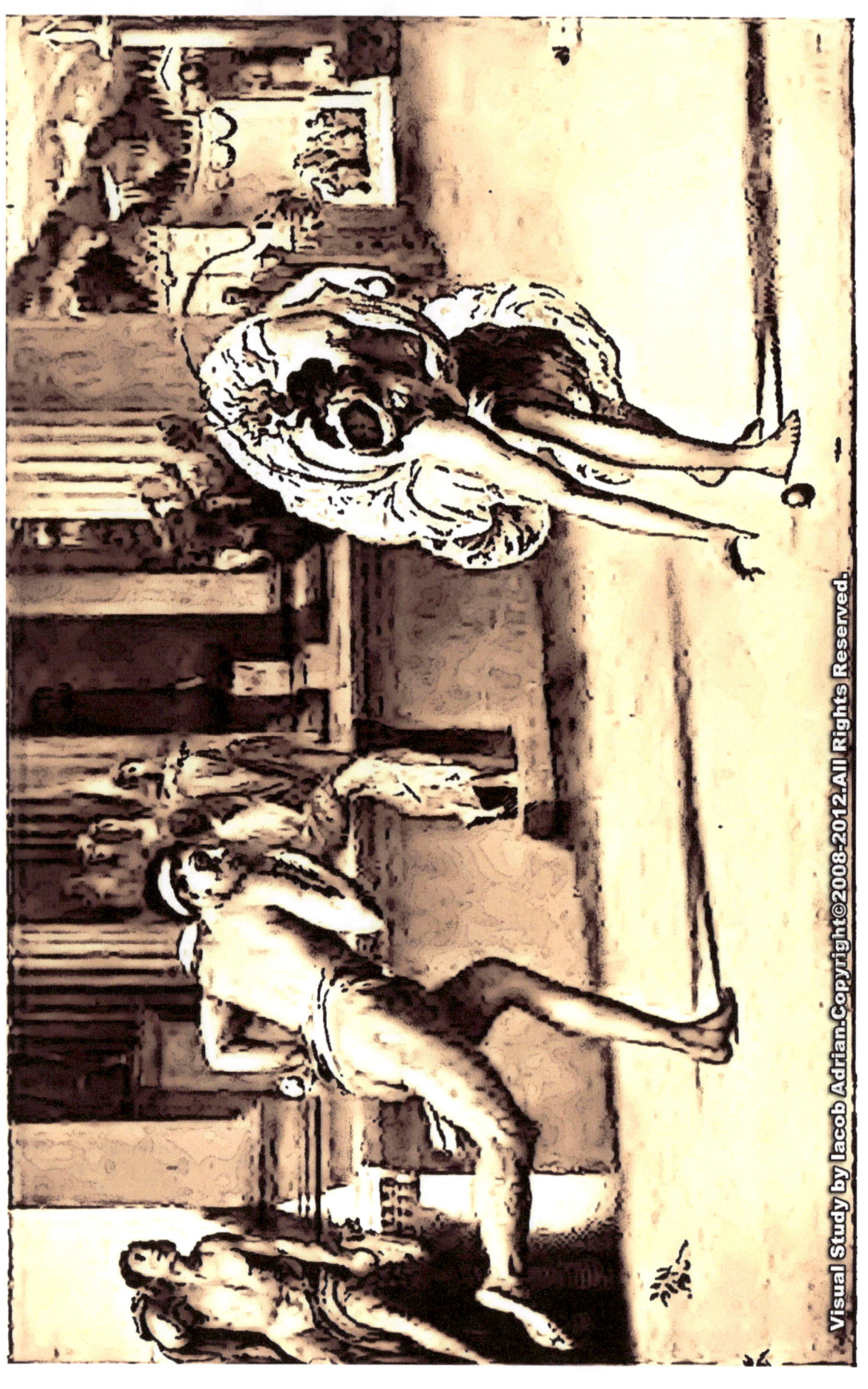

ATALANTA'S RACE

After the painting by Sir E. J. Poynter, P.R.A.

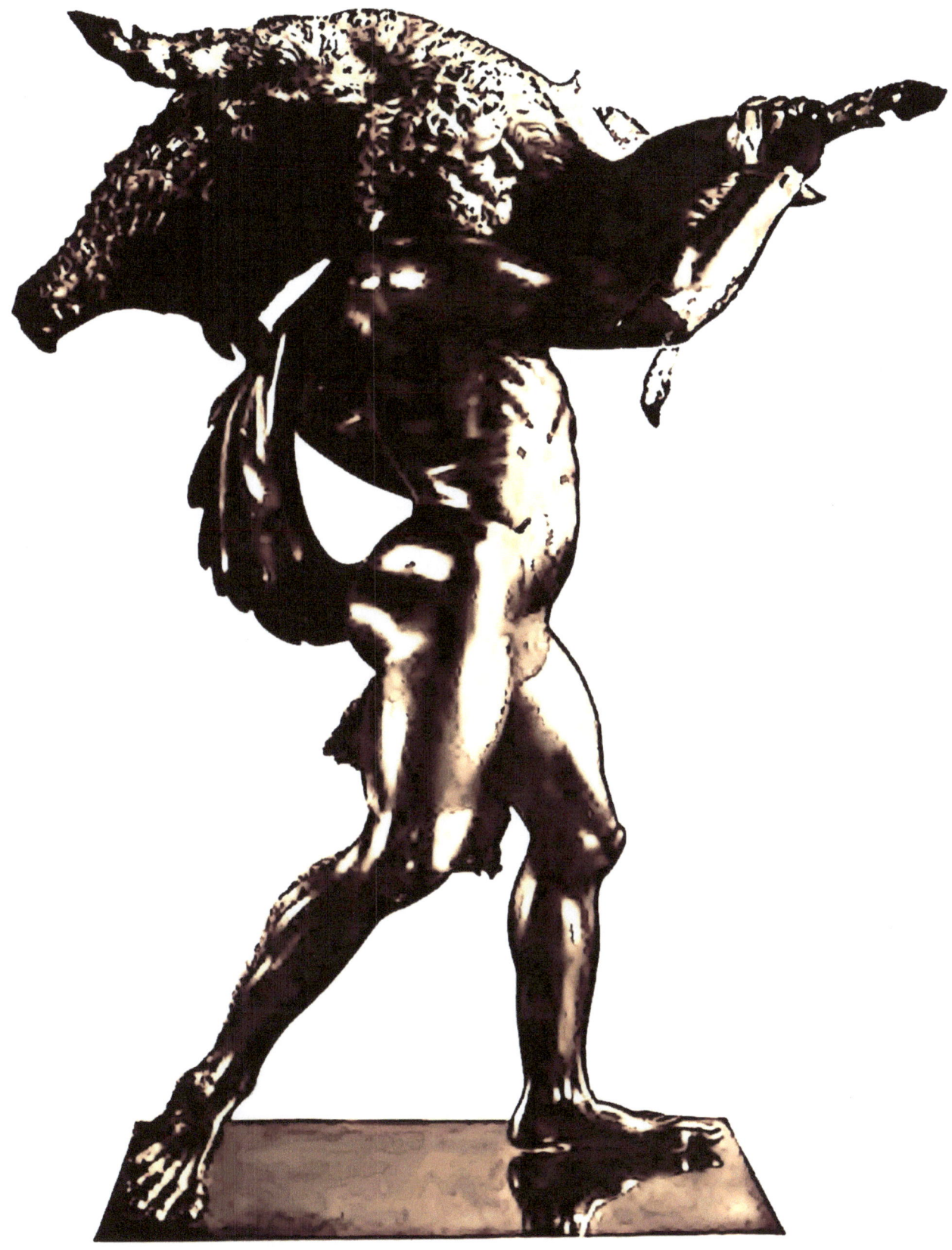

HERCULES AND THE BOAR

From the bronze by Jean de Bologne in the Louvre, Paris

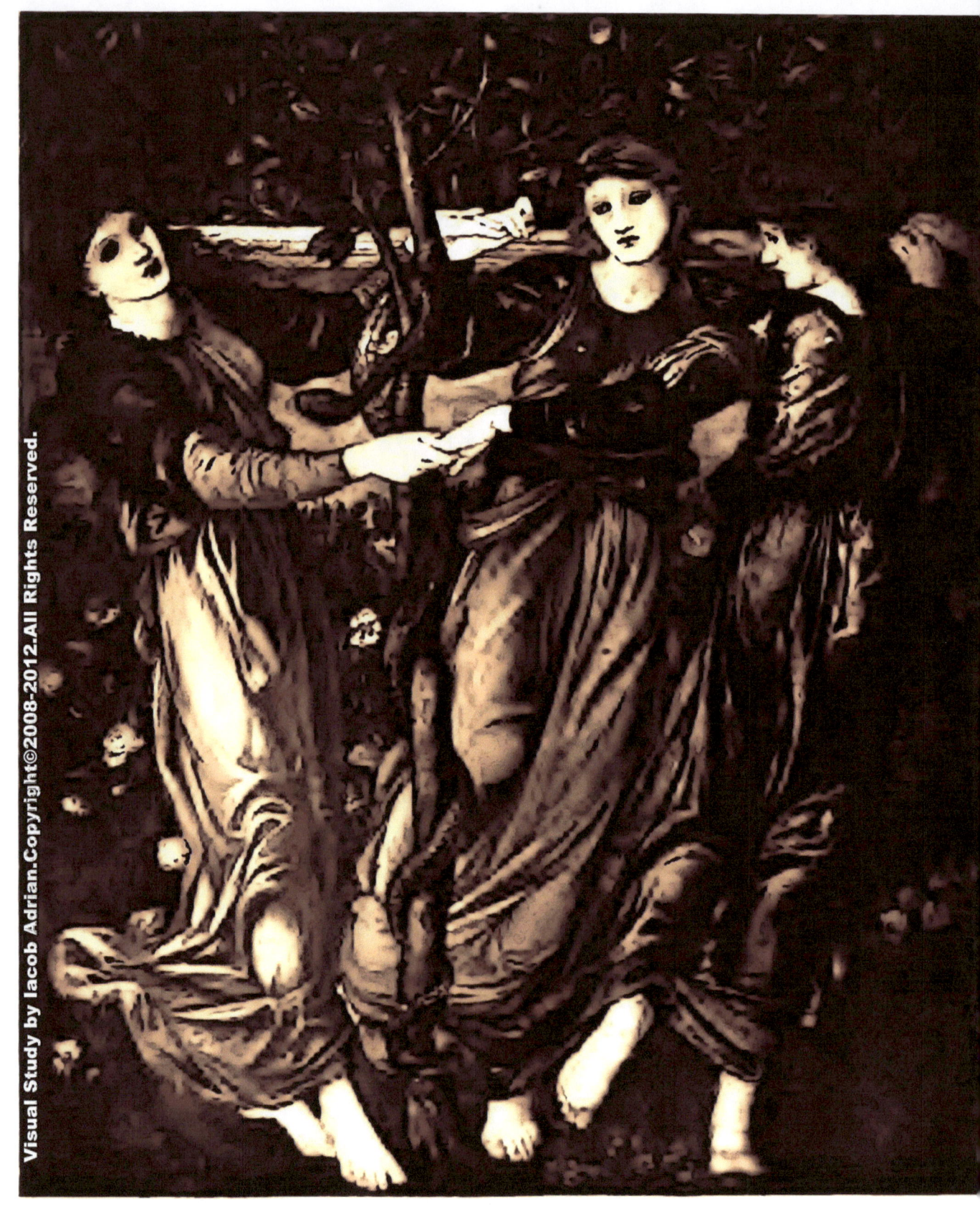

THE GARDEN OF THE HESPERIDES
By Sir Edward Burne-Jones

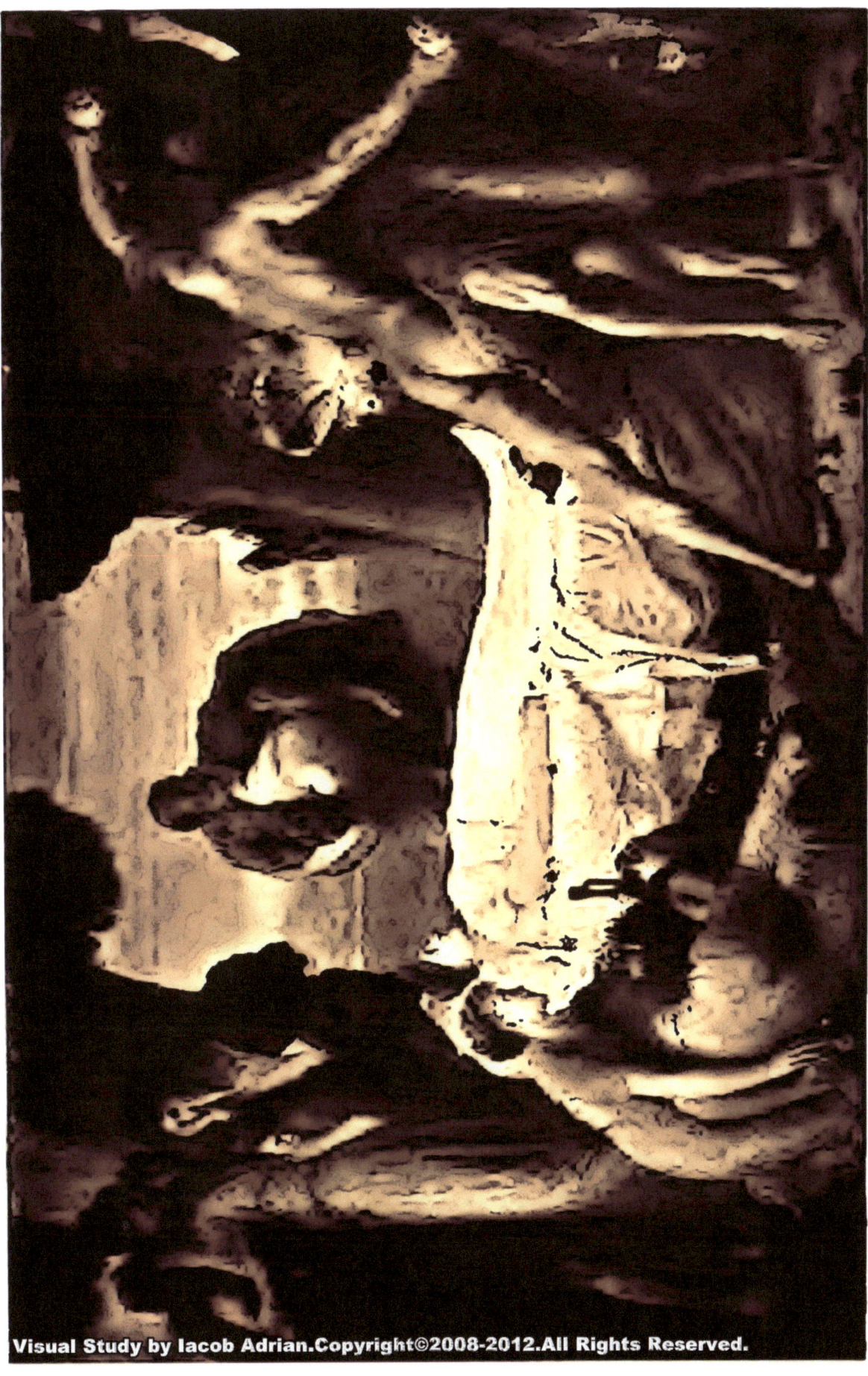

HERCULES WRESTLING WITH DEATH FOR THE BODY OF ALCESTIS

From the painting by Lord Leighton, P.R.A.

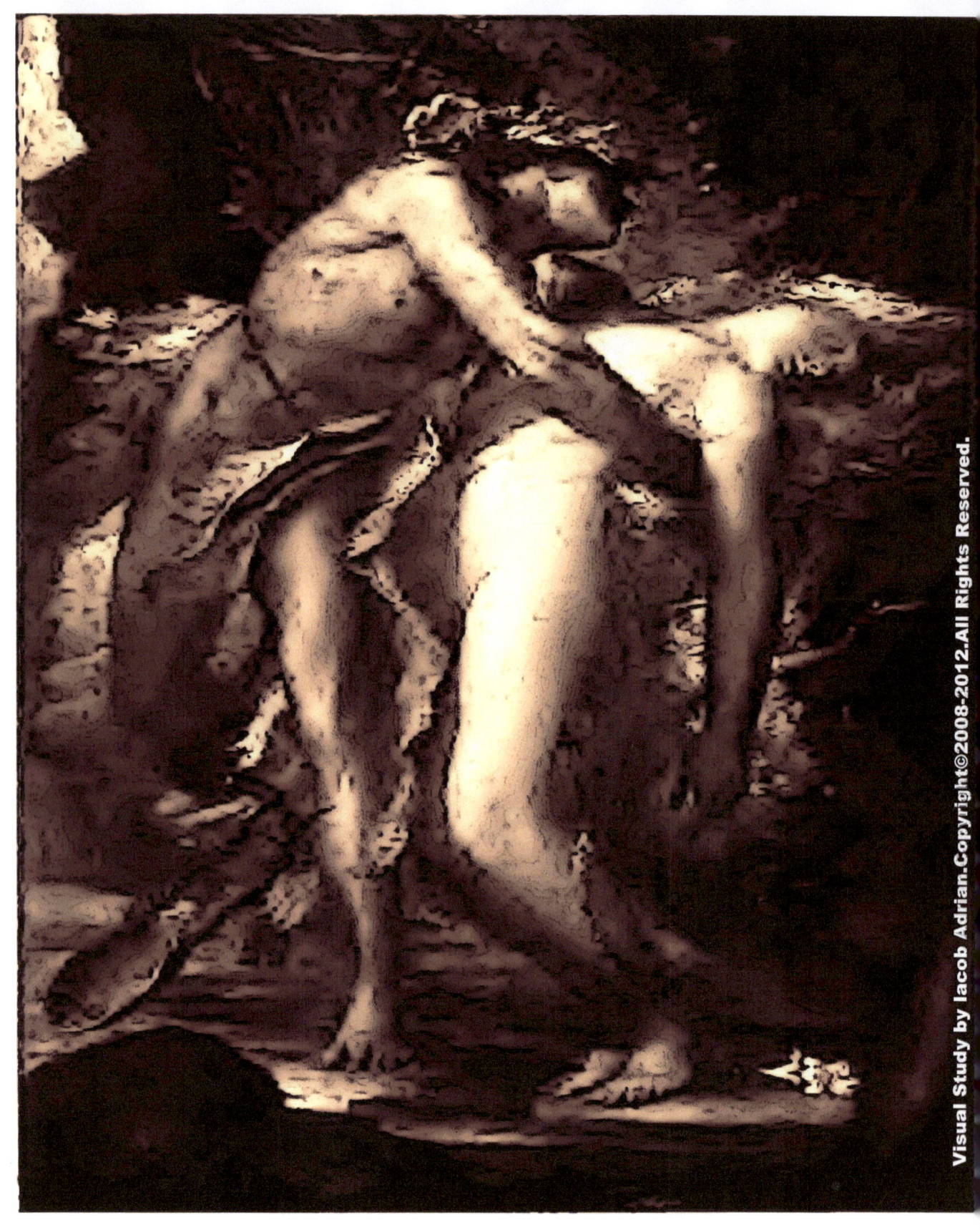

ORPHEUS AND EURYDICE

By G. F. Watts, R.A.

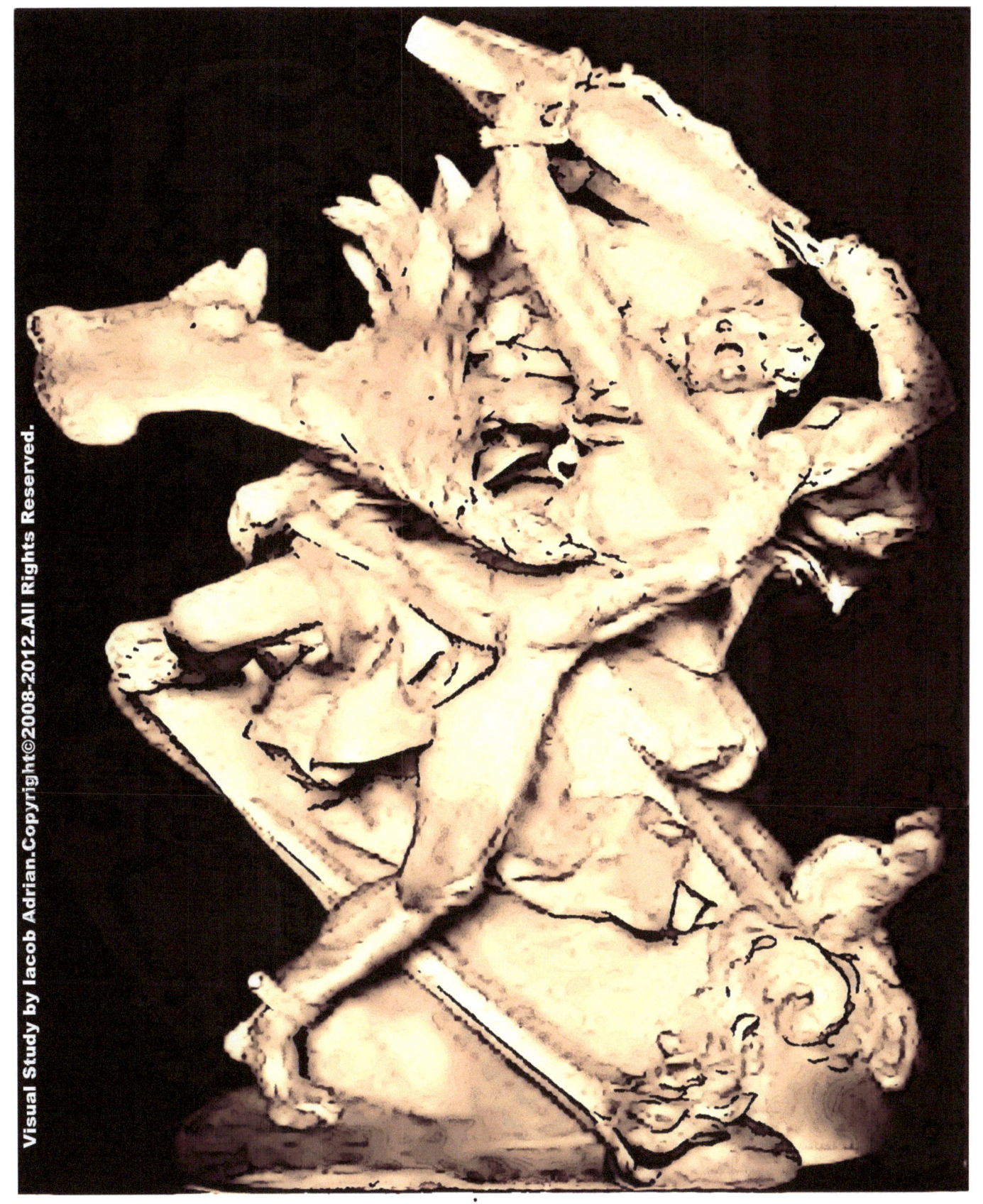

PROMETHEUS
From the sculpture by Puget

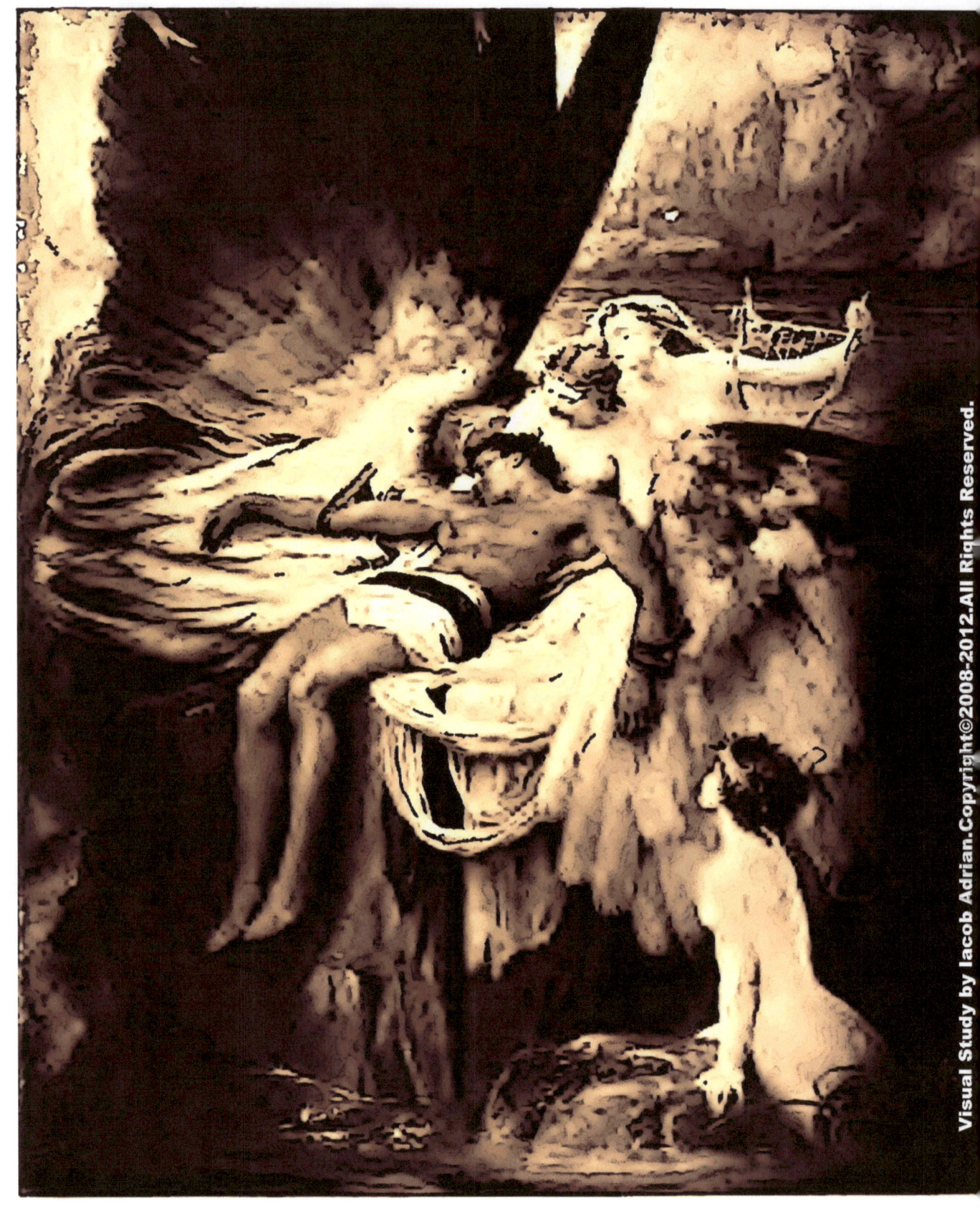

THE LAMENT FOR ICARUS

From the painting by Herbert J. Draper in the National (Tate) Gallery of British Art

ARIADNE IN NAXOS

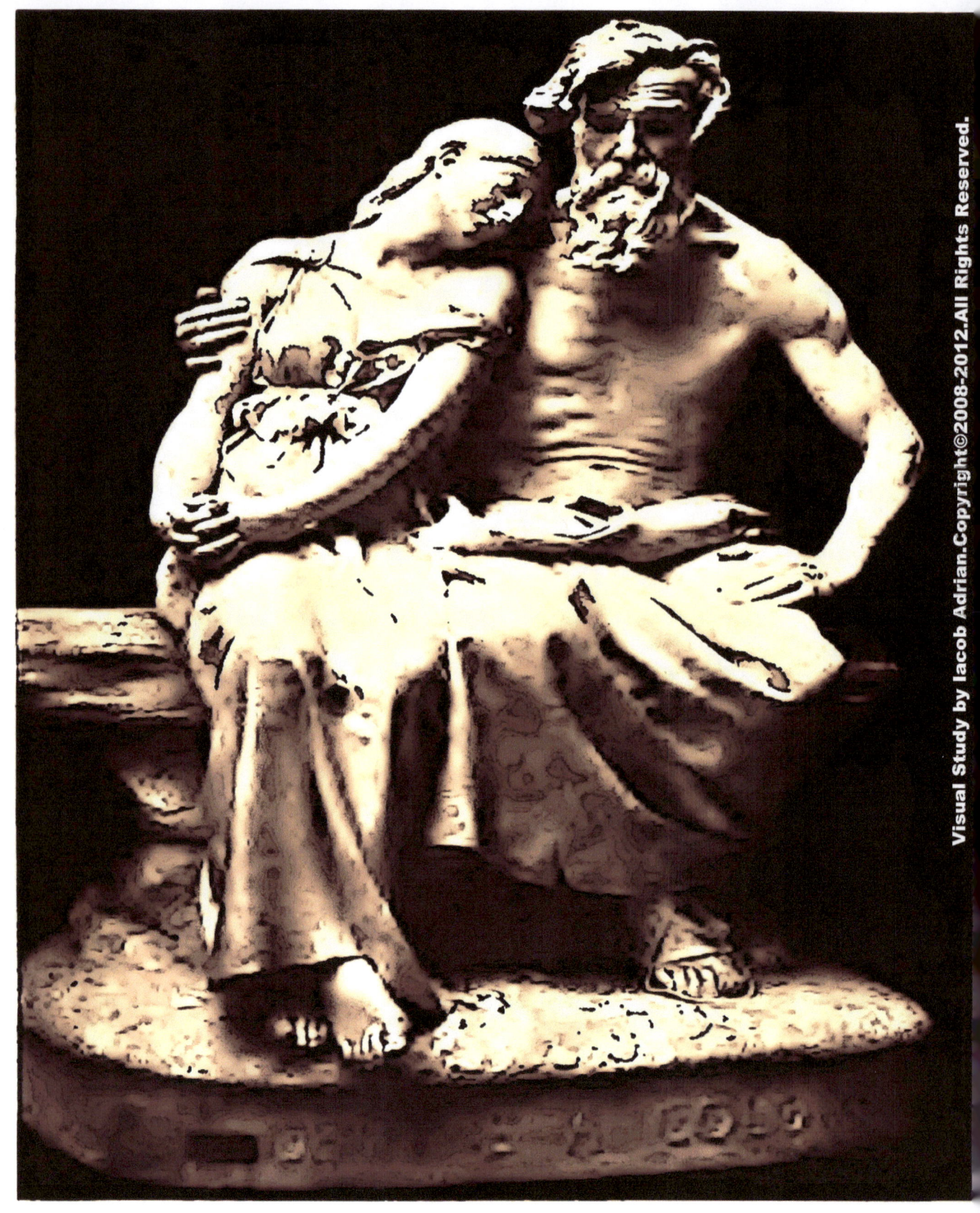

ŒDIPUS AT COLONOS

From the sculpture by Hugues in the Luxembourg, Paris

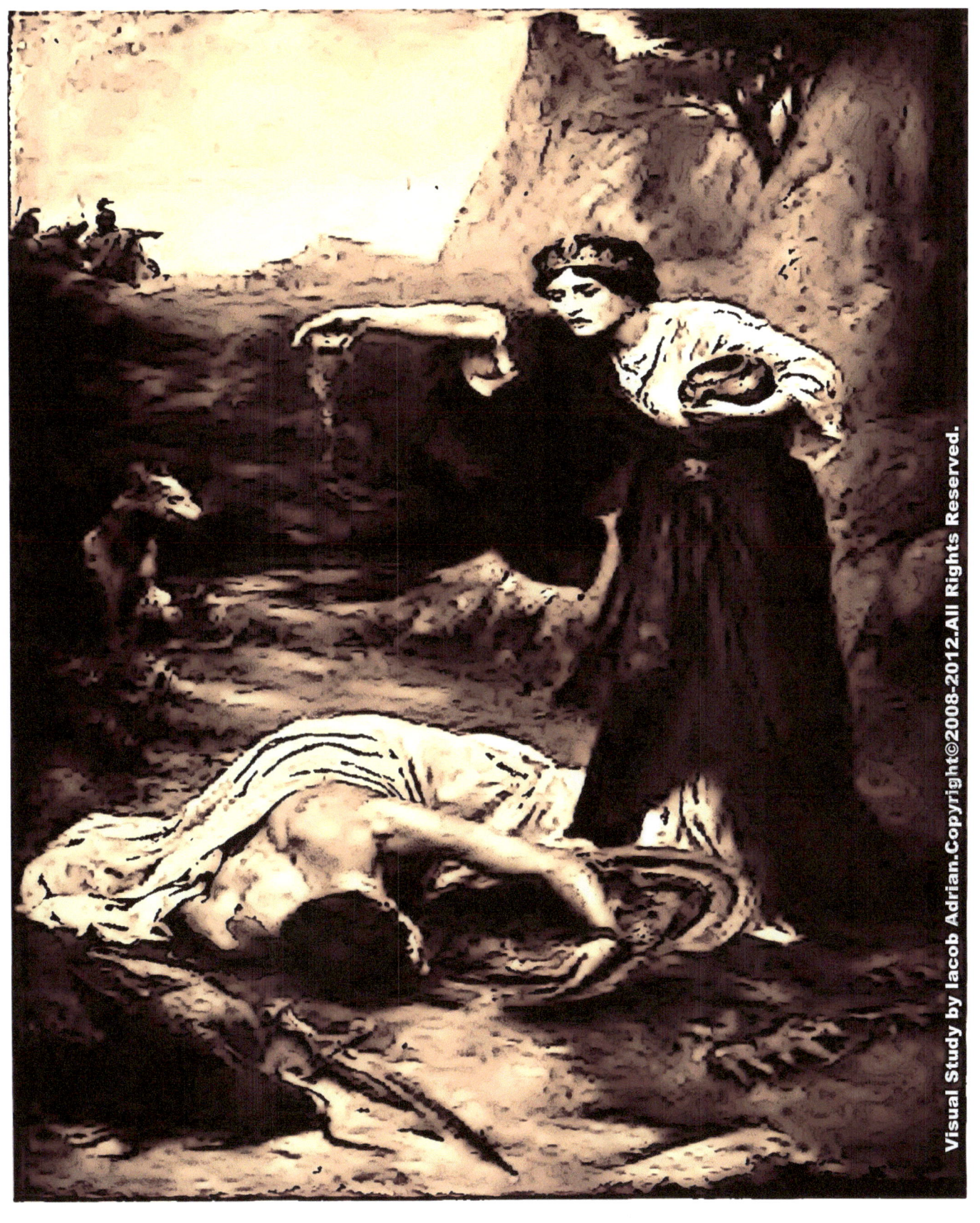

ANTIGONE STREWING DUST ON THE BODY OF POLYNEICES

From the painting by Victor J. Robertson.

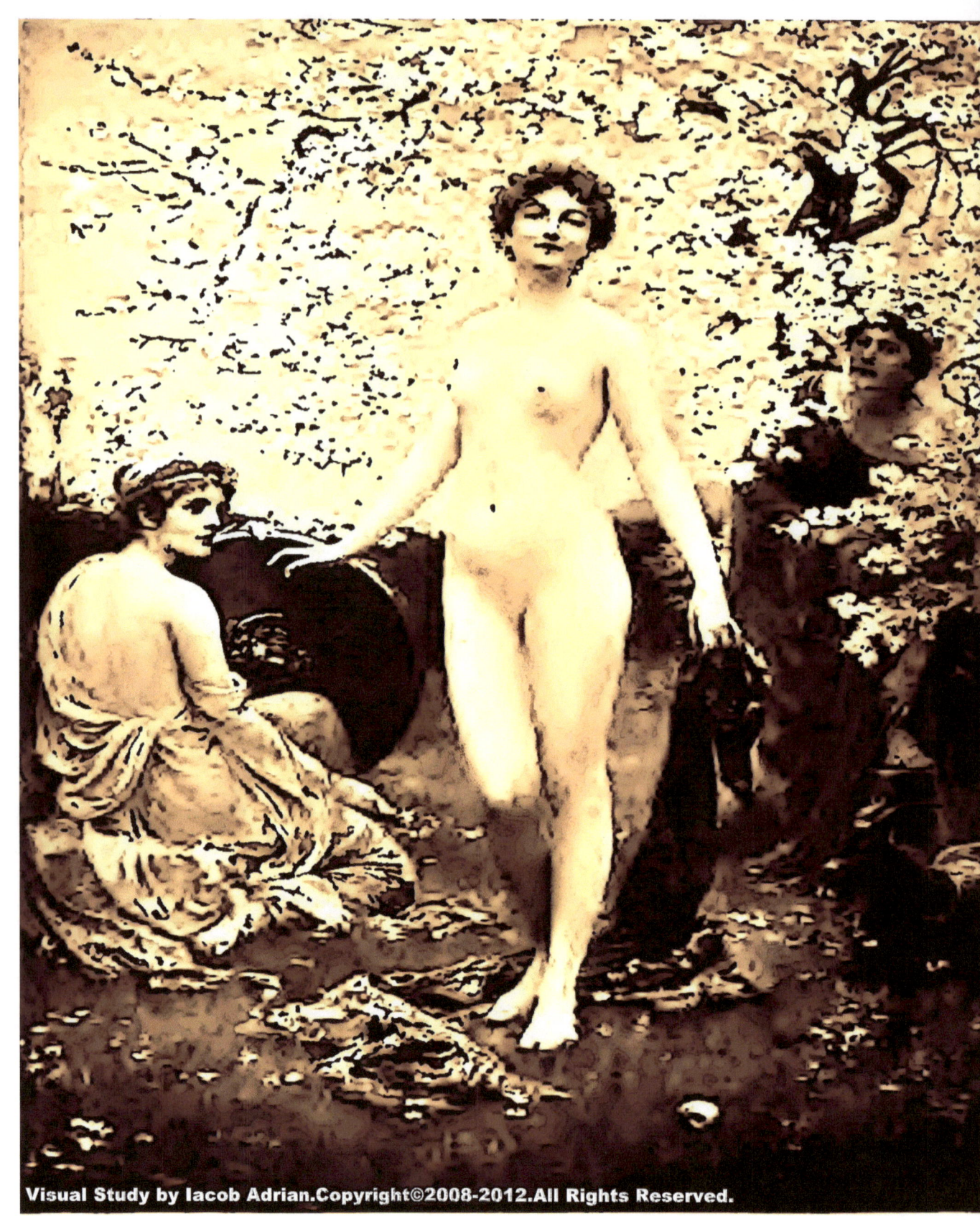

THE JUDGMENT OF PARIS
From the painting by Solomon J. Solomon, R.A.

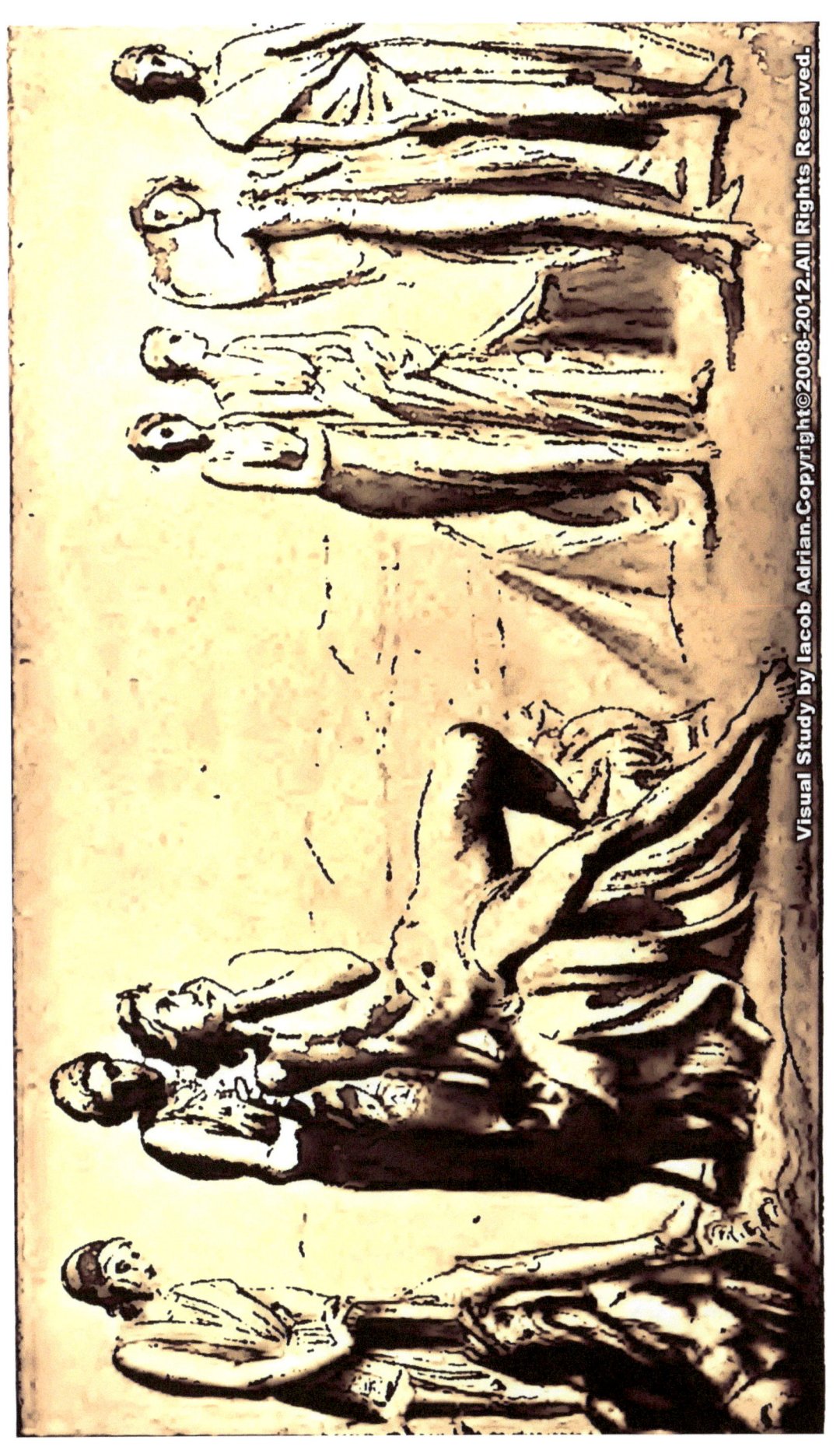

THE PARTING OF ACHILLES AND BRISEIS
By G. F. Watts, R.A.

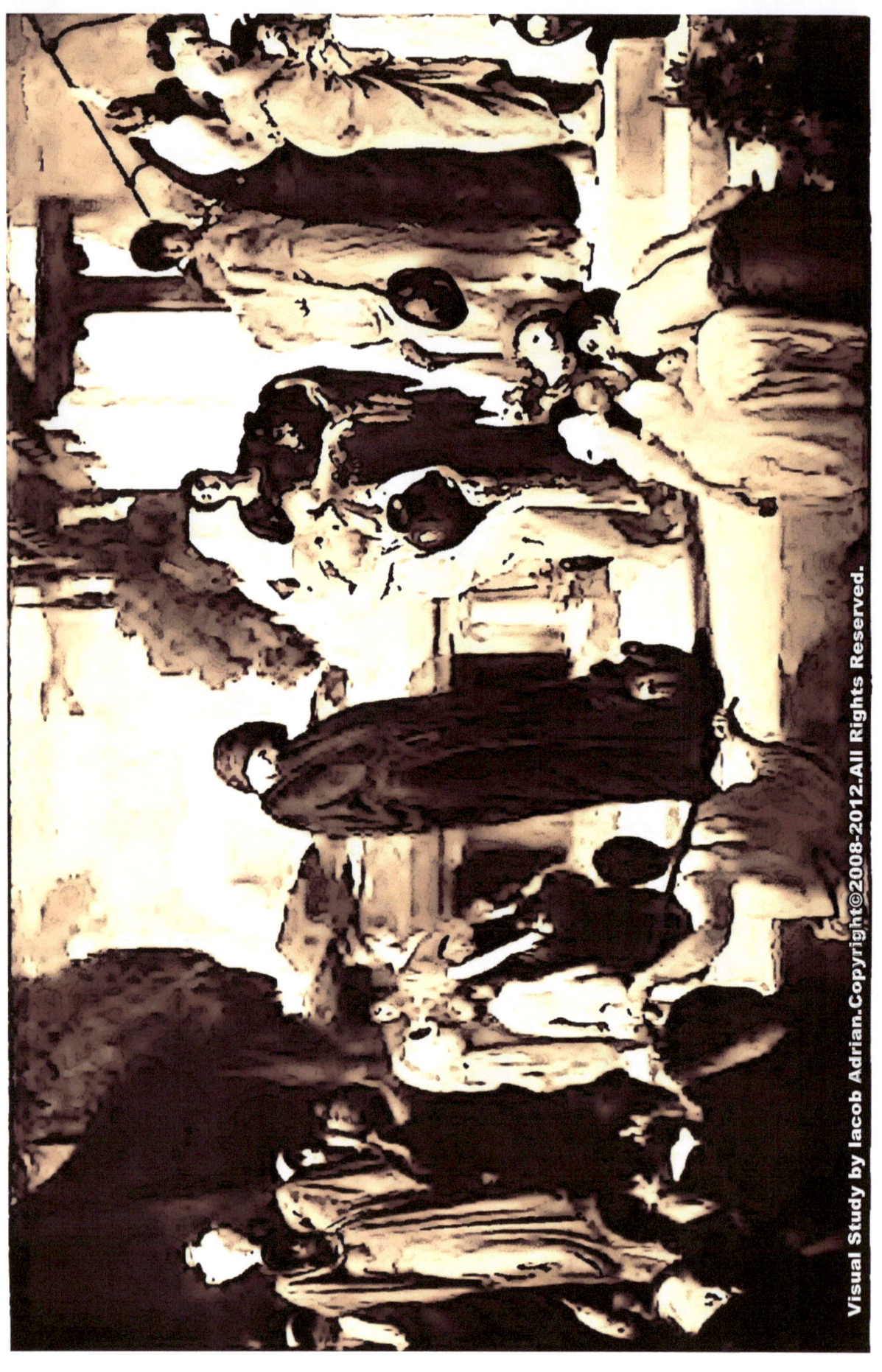

CAPTIVE ANDROMACHE

From the painting by Lord Leighton. P.R.A.

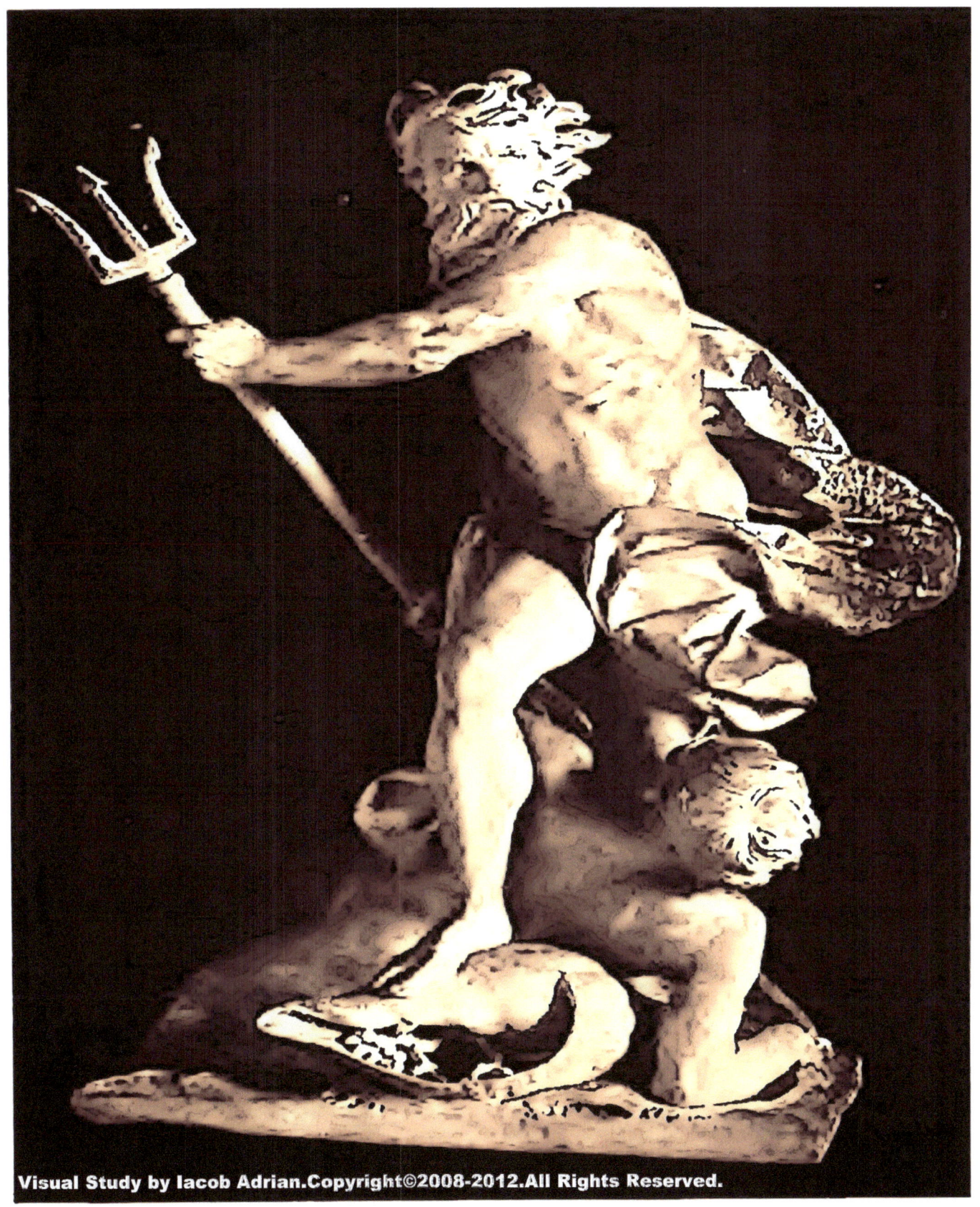

NEPTUNE
From the sculpture by Adam in the Louvre, Paris

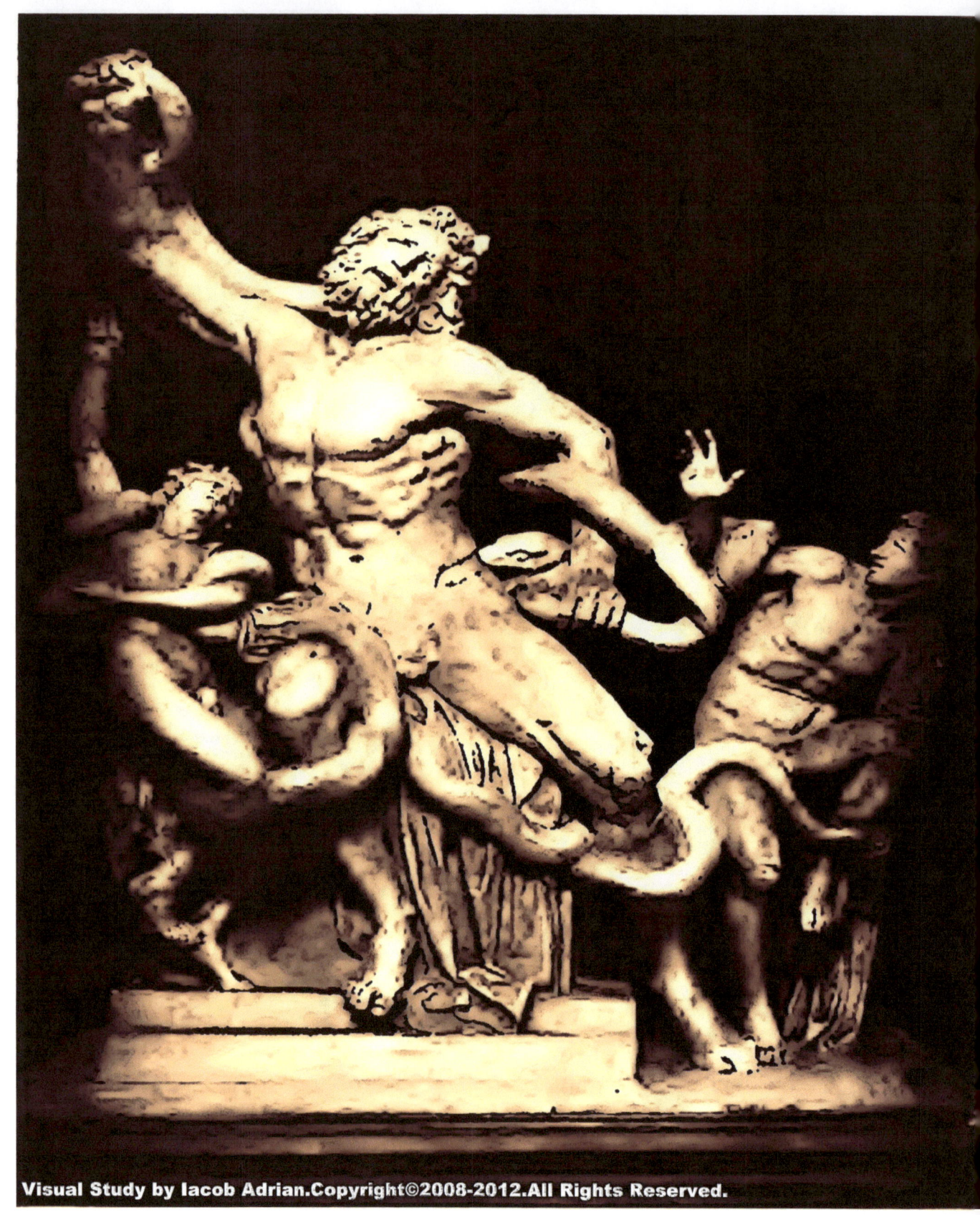

LAOCOON AND HIS SONS
From the sculpture in the Vatican Museum, Rome

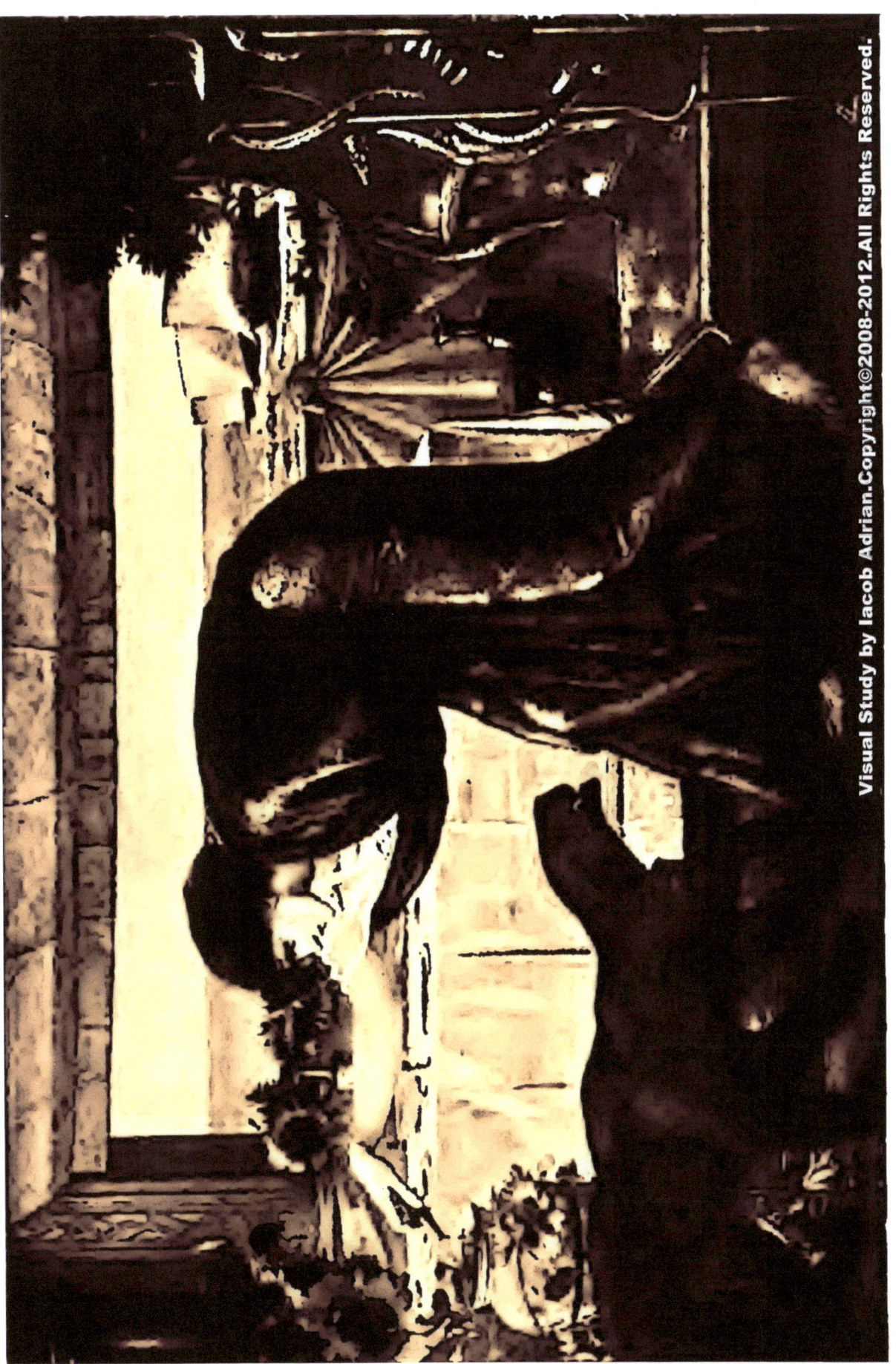

CIRCE
By Sir Edward Burne-Jones

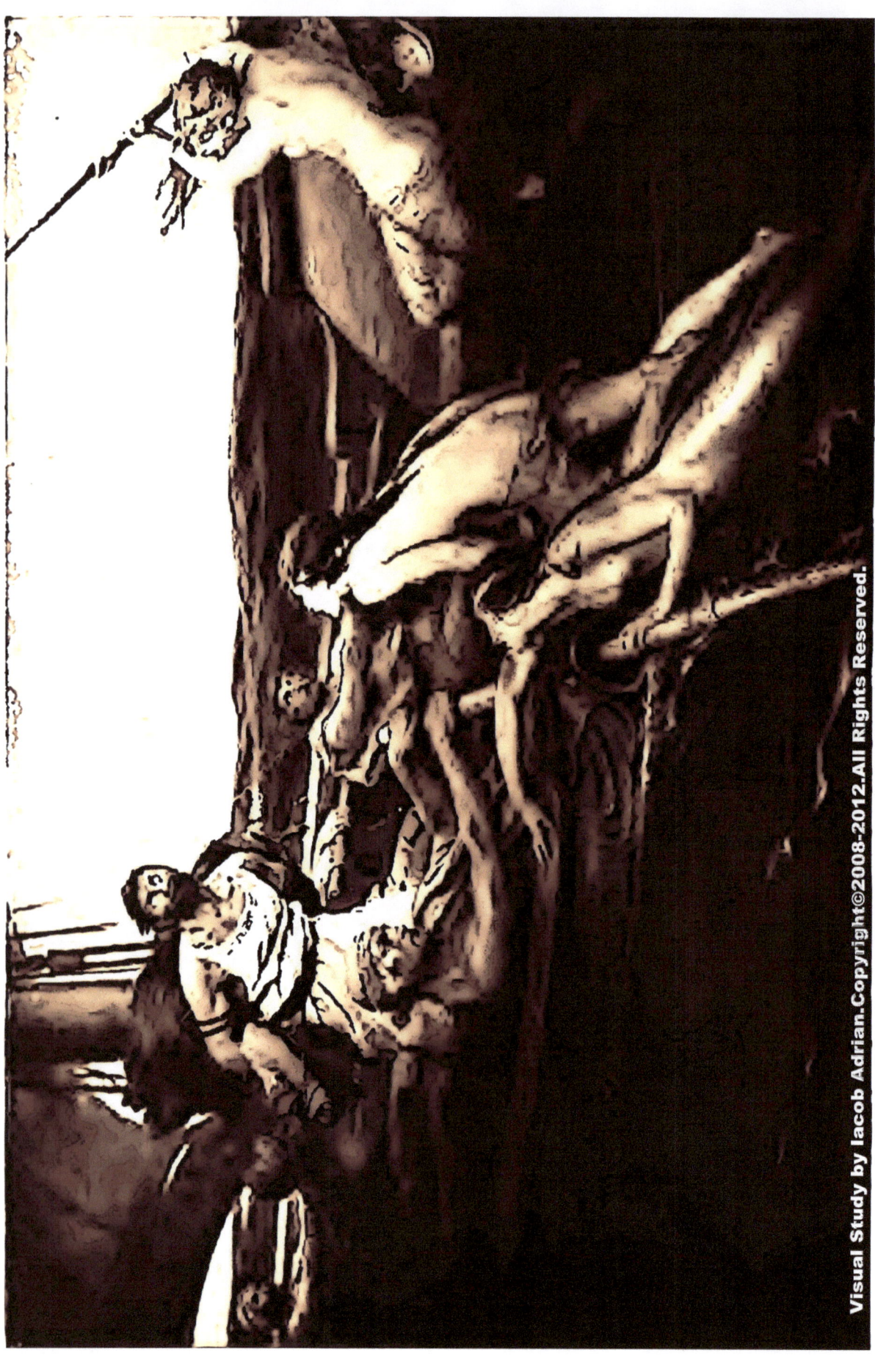

ULYSSES AND THE SYRENS. *By permission of the Corporation of Hull*

From the painting by Herbert J. Draper.

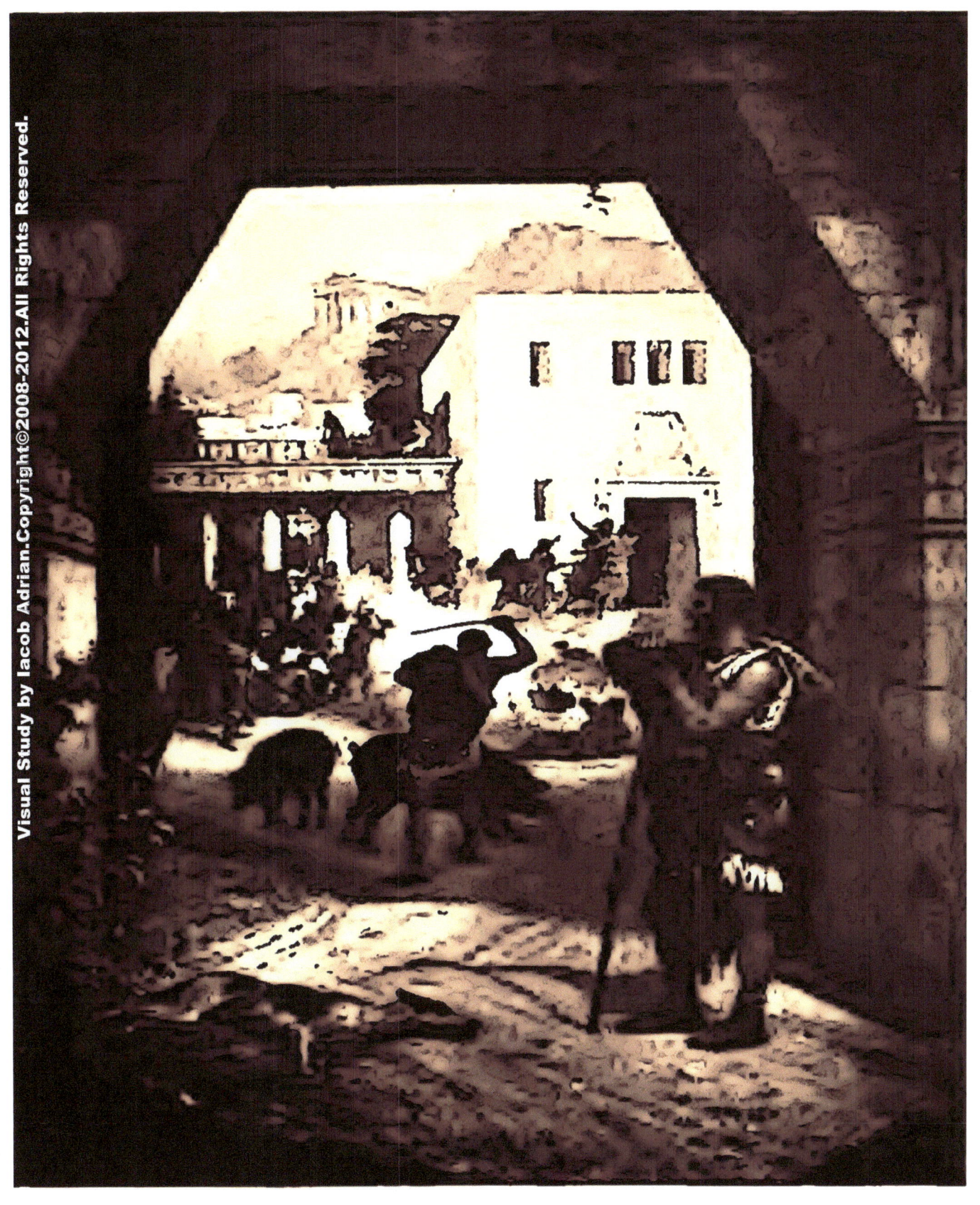

THE RETURN OF ULYSSES

From the painting by L. F. Schutzenberger

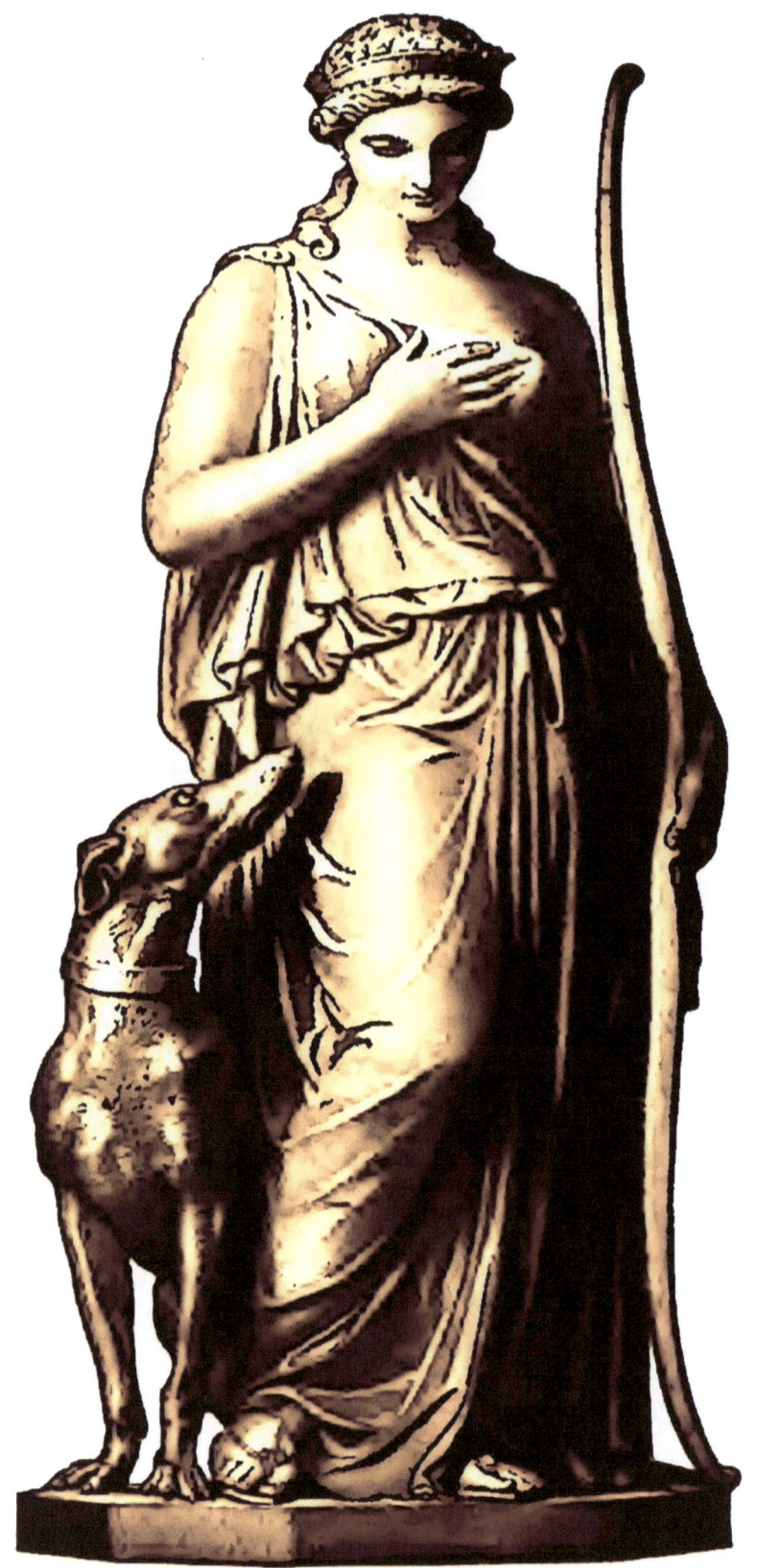

PENELOPE

After the statue by R. J. Wyatt in the possession of the late Queen Victoria

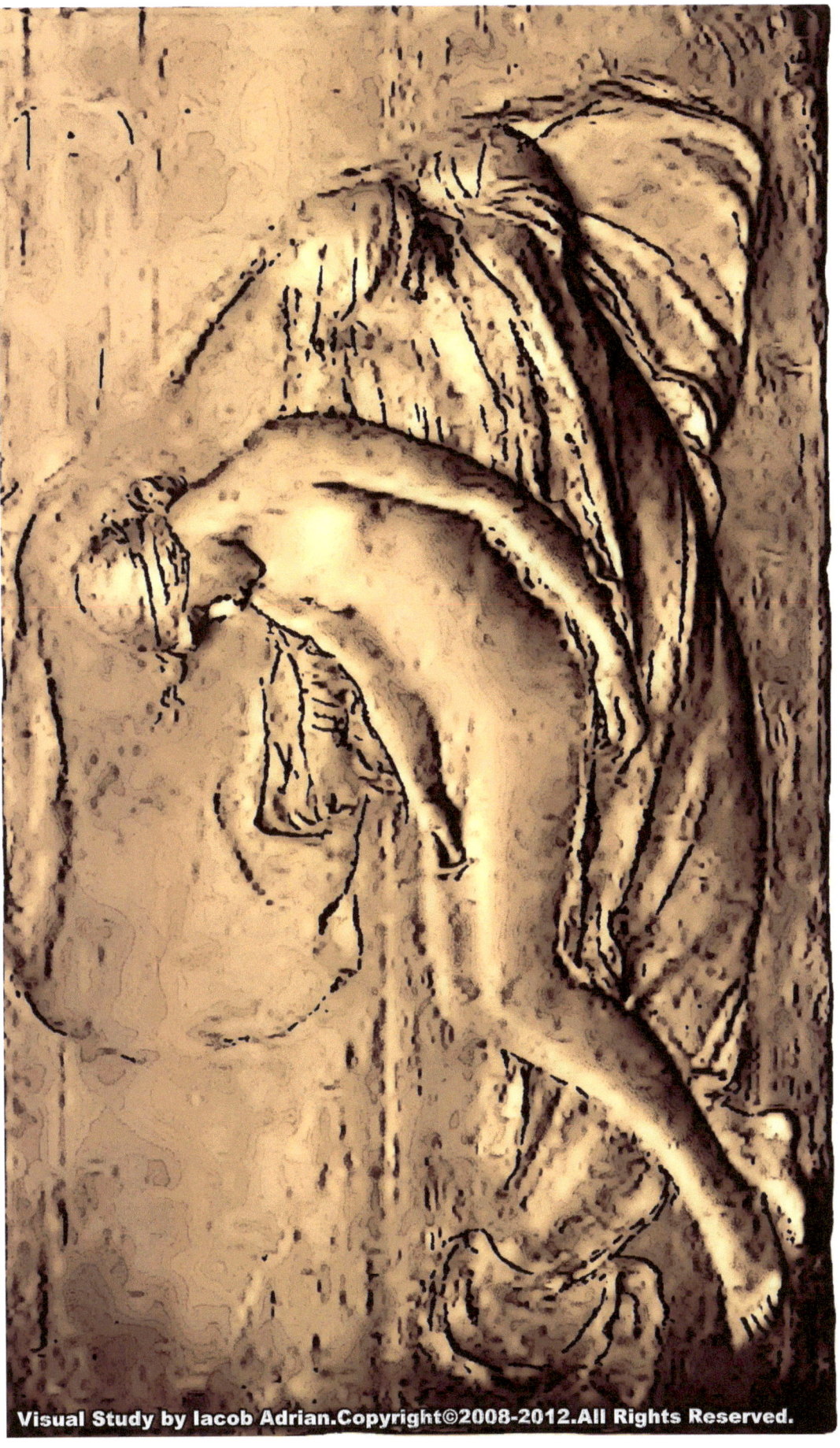

PSYCHE AND ZEPHYRUS
From the clay relief by Harry Bates

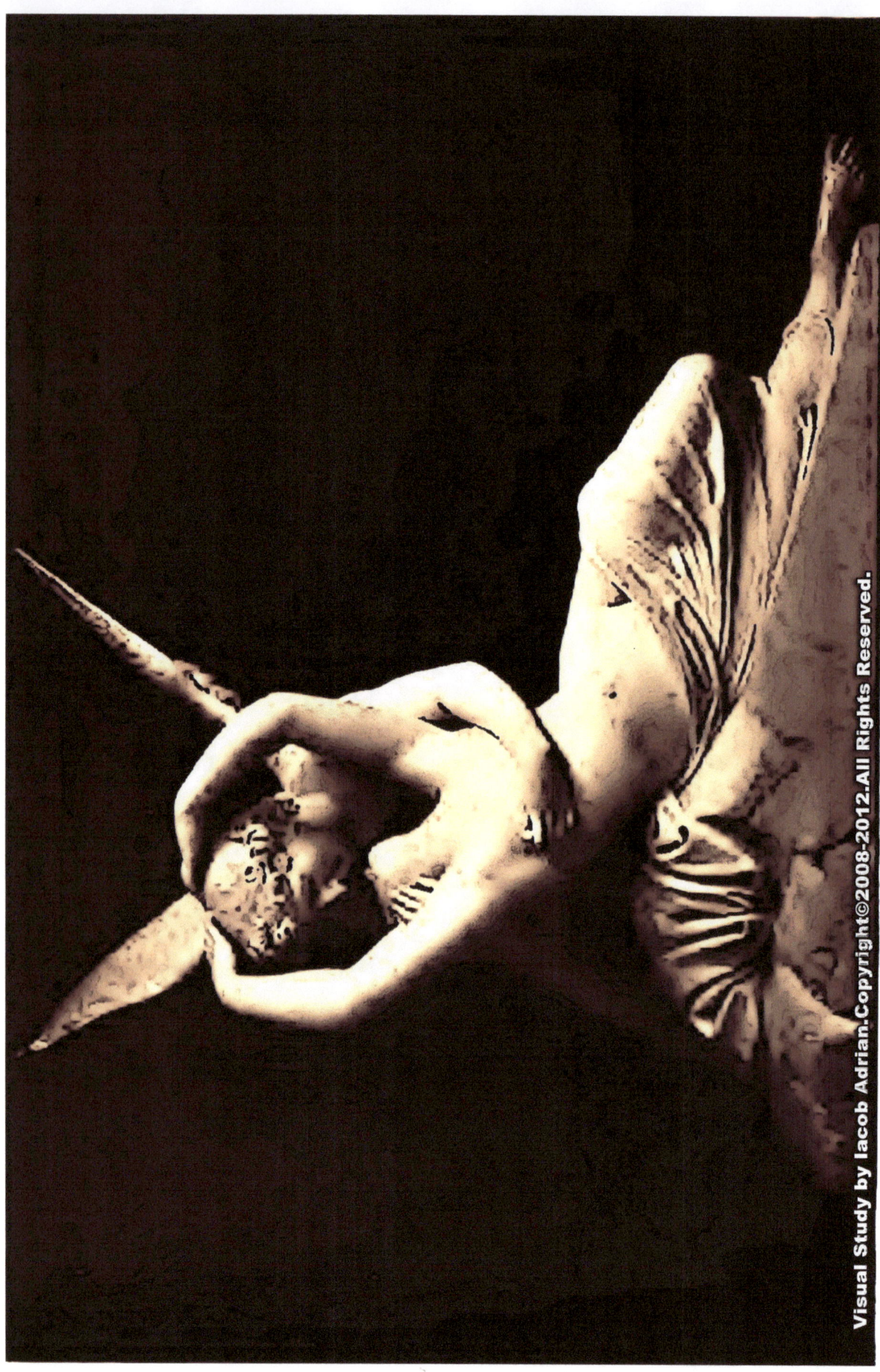

CUPID AND PSYCHE

From the marble sculpture by Canova

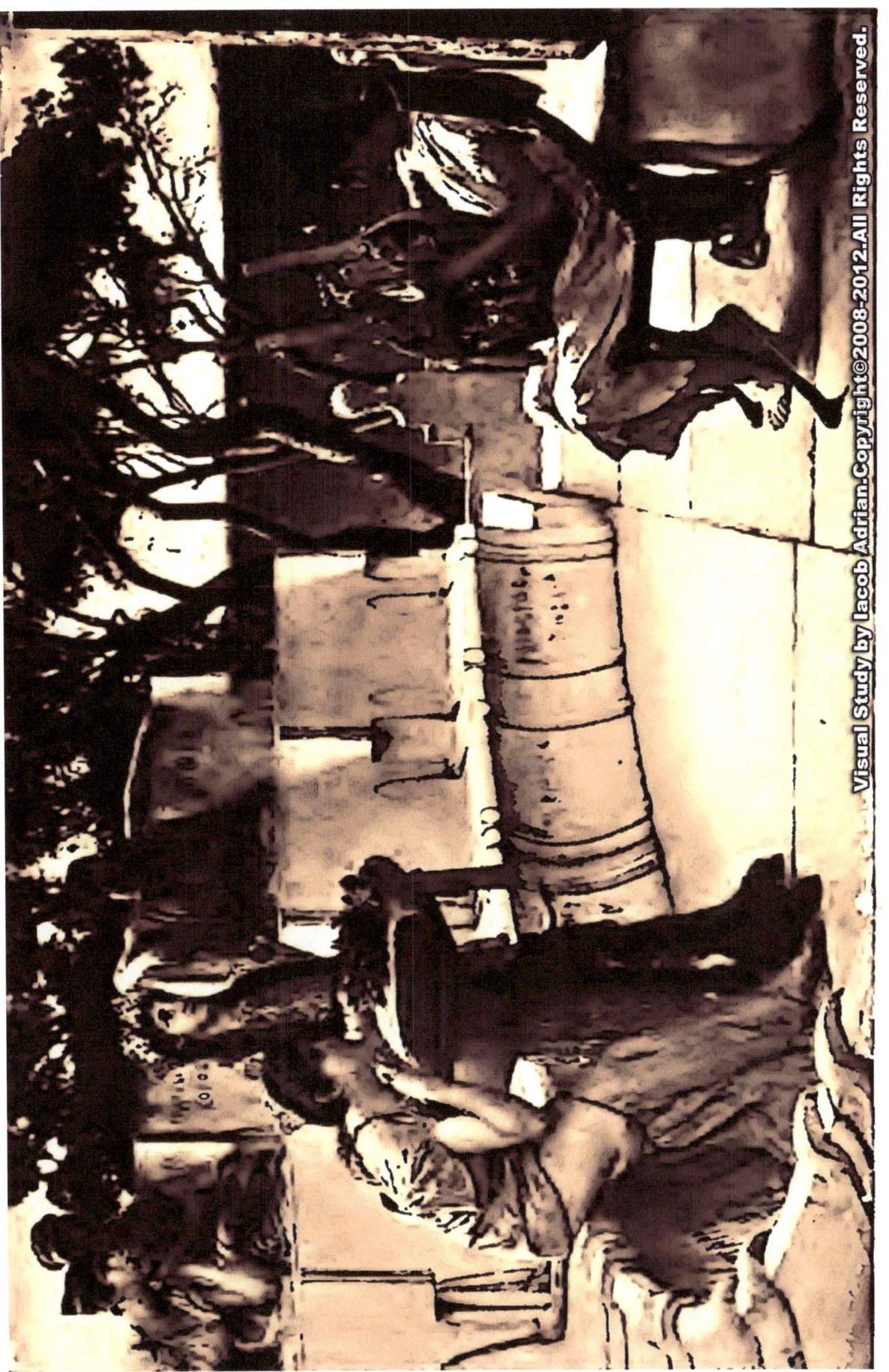

SAPPHO

From the painting by Sir L. Alma Tadema, R.A.

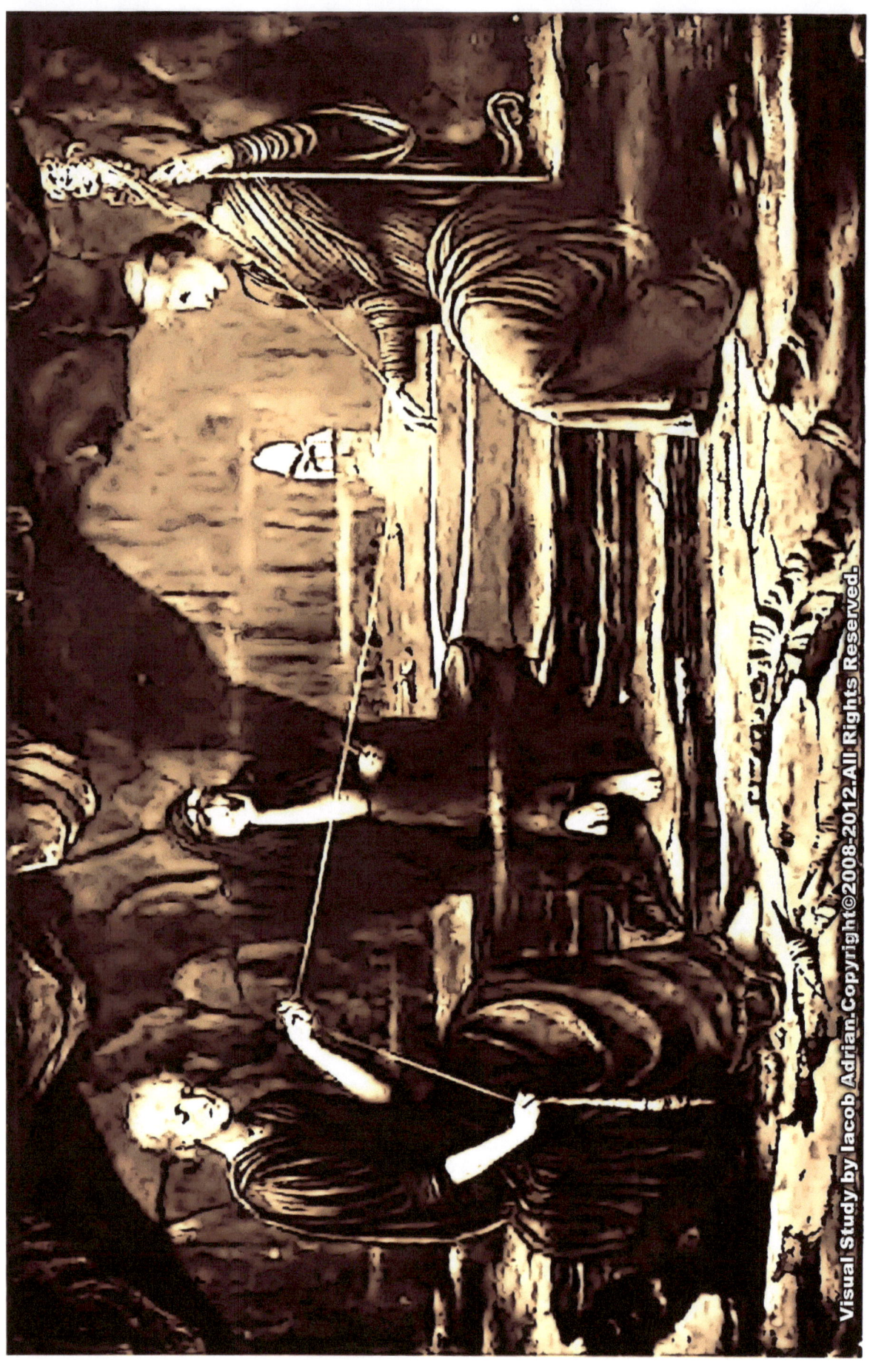

THE THREE FATES

From the painting—" A Golden Thread "—by J. M. Strudwick in the National (Tate) Gallery of British Art

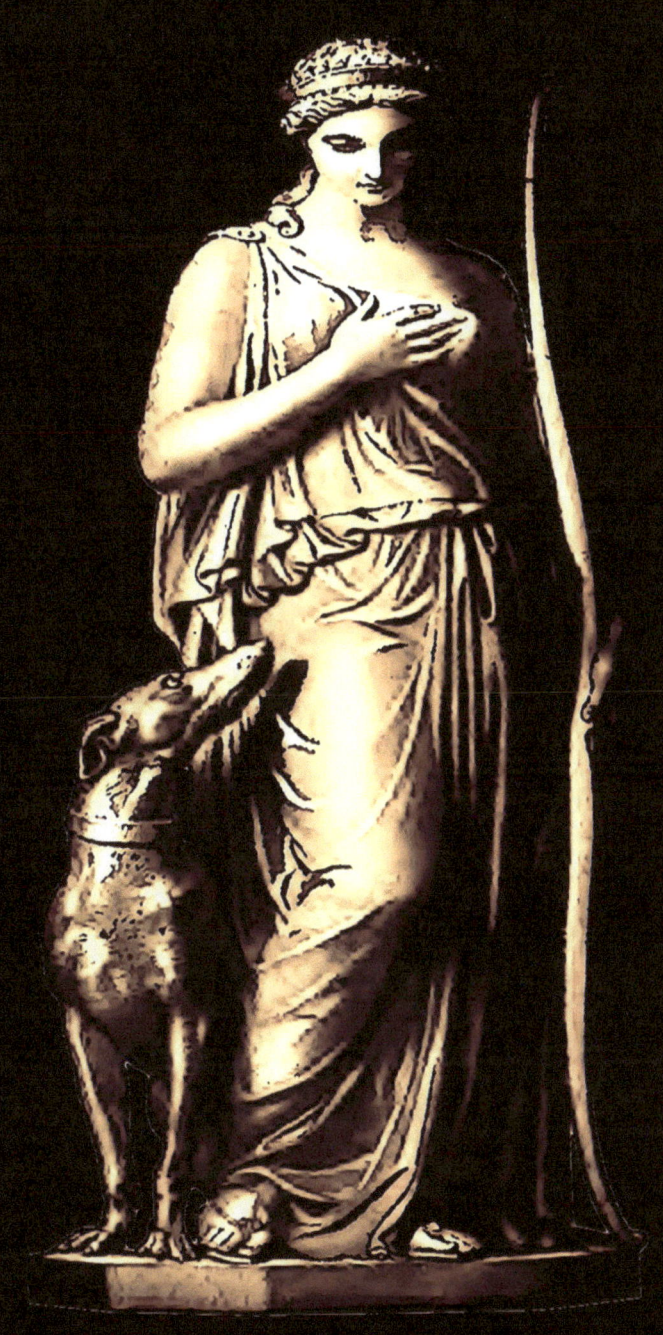

This documentary study use, combined in various proportions,
elements from the following categories, forms and subsets :
- fair use
- documentary
- documentary photography
- feature
- journalism
- arts journalism
- visual journalism
- photojournalism
- celebrity photography
in order to :
- employ material as the object of cultural critique ,
- quote to illustrate an argument or point ,
- use material in historical sequence,
providing independent opinion,
using photos, press articles, advertisements,
opinions of fans etc. ...

www.ingramcontent.com/pod-product-compliance
Lightning Source LLC
Chambersburg PA
CBHW051100180526
45172CB00002B/715